Schriften zu Gesundheit und Gesellschaft - Studies on Health and Society

Volume 1

Fortschreitende Digitalisierung, demographischer Wandel und komplexer werdende Umwelten stellen Wissenschaft und Gesellschaft vor neue Herausforderungen. Die tief greifenden Veränderungen betreffen in besonderem Maße auch den Bereich der Gesundheit. Eine Vielfalt wissenschaftlicher Disziplinen und Akteure aus allen gesellschaftlichen Bereichen sind gefordert, um die transformativen Prozesse der Gegenwart zu gestalten.

Die ceres **Schriften zu Gesundheit und Gesellschaft** bieten ein Forum für besonders gesellschaftsrelevante Fragen im Bereich der Gesundheit jenseits disziplinärer Grenzen. In ausgewählten Studien präsentieren sie fachübergreifende und translationale Analysen, Debatten und Konzepte zur partizipativen Gestaltung unserer Zukunft.

* * *

Digital developments, demographic change and increasingly complex environments pose all new challenges for science and society. These profound changes also, and in particular, affect health-related issues. It requires a variety of scientific disciplines and actors from all areas of society to shape the current transformative processes.

The ceres **Book Series on Health and Society** provides a forum for the discussion of particularly relevant societal challenges in the area of health, beyond disciplinary boundaries. In selected studies, the books of this series present interdisciplinary and translational analyses, debates and concepts, contributing to participative designs for our future.

More information about this series at http://www.springer.com/series/16017

Björn Schmitz-Luhn • Christiane Woopen
Editors

Justice over the Course of Life

Biographies in a Society of Long Lives

Springer

Editors
Björn Schmitz-Luhn
ceres
University of Cologne
Cologne, Germany

Christiane Woopen
ceres
University of Cologne
Cologne, Germany

Schriften zu Gesundheit und Gesellschaft - Studies on Health and Society
ISBN 978-3-030-86448-4 ISBN 978-3-030-86449-1 (eBook)
https://doi.org/10.1007/978-3-030-86449-1

This Springer imprint is published by the registered company Springer Nature Switzerland AG.
The registered company address is: Gewerbestrasse 11, 6330 Cham, Switzerland

Preface

Great advances in political and societal welfare, medicine, and public health have afforded our society a continuous rise in life expectancy, making the average age we can reach today the highest we have witnessed in history.

The increasing life spans mean substantial and systematic changes for many aspects of life, including education, work and employment, health services, and culture. Longer lives also transform our own perception of a typical lifetime, and affect our plans, imaginations, expectations, and needs at all ages. As all of us need to actively shape increasingly long lifetimes, and as the changes to all our areas of life continue to unfold, we are transforming into a society of long lives.

In shaping our lives, we depend on parameters that prevail in our society— which, in the long term, are themselves influenced by the very biographic realities and values the members of society create, develop, and elaborate. In addition, our lives are not only longer, but the way we age, our individual ideas of how to live our lives, our actions in their different stages, and our preferences in forming out our existence over the decades are becoming increasingly diverse. The concept of aging thus also embraces increasingly multifaceted aspects, making this new society of long lives one that is pluralistic, and characterized by diversity and individuality.

Today's historic freedom to shape our lives, however, comes along with a growing and increasingly complex responsibility: Individual responsibility calls us to fill the increased lifetimes with aims, meaning, and answers to what we expect a "successful" or "fulfilling," "flourishing" life to be—and the farther we can plan ahead for our own later life, the more aspects and chances have to be weighed and considered for our decisions. Our values and preferences also change over the course of our lifetimes, as we may adjust our convictions and aims to change opportunities and conditions.

Alongside, a collective responsibility arises to integrate our different designs of longer lives with a functioning society in which individual interests are brought to collective concordance, in order to guarantee maximum freedom for all. While we react to the chance of longer lives, we also create realities and values every day with our decisions and plans by which we, in turn, collectively influence societal concepts and frameworks. As the changes brought about by longer lifetimes continue and become more pertinent, this also includes safeguarding and renegotiating our collective values as well as existing concepts and principles of societal coexistence.

In light of all these changes and challenges to shape our society, one principle seems to stand out: The longer our lives and the more important our responsibility to consider our later lives, the more fundamental is the role of safeguarding justice to and between generations. It is not only an enabling condition for secure and rational planning ahead, but also a foundation for a sound and resilient order of society in which a growing number of generations who are alive at the same time, will coexist. A just and equitable social system is a natural prerequisite for meeting the evolving changes by the guarantee of human rights, security, and fairness, while enabling all generations to react to them with developing evermore pluralistic and individual lifestyles.

In this volume, the authors highlight the principle of justice from the perspectives of most pertinent areas of change and challenges associated with an aging society. The chapters in this book, therefore, focus on three major aspects of justice in an aging society: Planning ahead, life-long engagement, and participation, as well as medical care and health literacy.

In part one, justice is examined as a condition for successful advanced life planning and social security schemes. Old-age pension schemes are a most tangible example. Additionally, social security mechanisms guaranteeing good medical care at a higher age are considered elementary. Philosopher *Dieter Birnbacher* shows, based on *John Rawls'* Theory of Justice, and looking at other EU states' social systems, that it is primarily an older generation being at the center of social policy issues, whereas a younger generation tends to be neglected. Empirical psychologist *Klaus Rothermund* presents factors that influence people's preparations for old age, analyzing the concept of old-age preparation as well as specific measures, e.g., regarding health planning and housing. He also shows the difference in their intensity depending on the phase of life people are in but also on gender, age, and income. Regarding age-related discrimination in social security systems, legal scientist and philosopher *Stefan Huster* offers a new perspective by showing that age as such is a particularly egalitarian criterion for legal differentiation, since everyone will have a certain age at some point in time—but points out that accordingly, age-related discrimination is seldom based directly on age but rather found in the shape of unjust enabling provisions of social security.

Another fundamental part of human life is social engagement. Part two is therefore dedicated to justice as an enabling principle for life-long social participation, highlighting both inter-generational exchange and coexistence as well as work as one of the major uses of time and attainment in human life. *Peter Dabrock* puts the relationship between freedom, social participation, and justice in the center, exploring a synchronic perspective of the relationships between the age groups on theological grounds. He points out that justice, solidarity, and care are the factors guaranteeing individual and social benefits, especially within a society facing demographic changes. *Mathilde Niehaus* develops models to strengthen inter-generational fairness in the workplace, working out the relationships between work, health, productivity, and age, with particular respect to older workers. *Jutta Allmendinger* and *Ellen von den Driesch* take a look at the differing employment situation between men and women, as well as the distribution of work-related activities and duties over the lifetime. They come up with a comprehensive proposal to better allocate work-related efforts over the lifetime according to the different specific demands in various phases of life and with a view to longer lives and active periods of employment.

In its third part, the book deals with inter-generational and social justice for medical care and health literacy. Health awareness has gained considerable importance in all generations, and has also become an important consideration for people wanting to live longer lives while avoiding age-related ailments. Psychologist *Ralf Schwarzer* debates possible motivational and behavioral support in health behavior changes and the ways in which individuals could be giving an incentive to reduce health-compromising behaviors. However, as the age of the population increases, age-related conditions, e.g., Alzheimer's disease, may also become more common. Legal scientist *Reinhard Damm* takes a closer look at self-determination and care in people affected, punctuating the specific legal problems regarding care-related decision-making of very young and very old people, and advocating further discussion about the calibration of self-determination and care. Regarding health literacy and public enablement for health, *Kristine Sørensen* presents the findings of the European Health Literacy Project, which measured health literacy in eight European countries, and calls for the involvement of health professionals as well as patients and citizens, the redesign of health infrastructure, and further investment in health literacy activities. *Oliver Gröne* continues to carve out the achievements of patient involvement, citing quality improvements in clinical effectiveness, safety, and patient centeredness.

The treatises of this collective volume have been first made on the occasion of the inaugurate conference of the Cologne Center of Ethics, Rights, Economics, and Social Sciences of Health back in September 2014. They haven't lost any of their topicality, and continue, updated where affected by the ongoing debate, to highlight important aspects of the dynamic discussion to which we hope to contribute with this work. It aims to clarify and carve out some of the most significant effects and requirements brought about by an aging society. We hope that they succeed in pointing to possible solutions, necessary discussions, and impulses on how to safeguard and shape a just and secure social future for both old and young.

Cologne, Germany
May 2021

Björn Schmitz-Luhn
Christiane Woopen

Contents

How Fair Is the German Old-Age Pension System? 1
Dieter Birnbacher

Who Cares for What? Determinants of Preparation for Old Age Across the Life Course 13
Klaus Rothermund

Age Categories in Social Security Systems 25
Stefan Huster

Life Course and Social Participation: (Not Only) a Question of Fairness 37
Peter Dabrock

Fair Participation for Aging Employees at the Workplace 45
Mathilde Niehaus

Becoming Motivated and Competent to Perform Health-Enhancing Behaviors 51
Ralf Schwarzer

Autonomy and Care in the Law of the Human Biography 63
Reinhard Damm

The Extra Years: Creating More Opportunities for Women and Men by Redistributing (Working) Time 87
Jutta Allmendinger and Ellen von den Driesch

Health Literacy in Europe: The Concept, Its Impact and Application . . 99
Kristine Sørensen

Patient Involvement in Health Care: Conceptualisation, Measurement, Uptake and Future Improvement 107
Oliver Gröne

How Fair Is the German Old-Age Pension System?

Dieter Birnbacher

1 Introduction

In the twenty-first century, the demand for social justice is an increasingly universal demand for the organisation of societies. This demand is a more or less natural development from liberal civil right. If civil rights that were hard-fought by the Enlightenment, such as the right of freedom of opinion, freedom of association, freedom of religion and free development of one's personality, are to become effective under real social conditions, more is required than a legal guarantee of these rights. Also required is the legal guarantee of the means for making use of these freedoms. "Creating effectiveness" of civil liberties requires social rights that ensure that everyone has at least the minimum resources required to utilise *in concreto* the rights granted *in abstracto*.

The further development of civil liberties into social rights that "make them effective" is a world historic process. It is shown in the historical sequence of political constitutions, the catalogues of human rights and not least in the historically changing understandings of the ethical-political basic concept of human dignity. While for those who pioneered the concept of human dignity during the Enlightenment focused on liberties and other defensive rights, in the nineteenth century, particularly through the labour movements, the idea of human dignity was enriched with social rights, such as the right to minimum subsistence and healthcare and the right to humane working and living conditions.

Therefore, it is no coincidence that "social justice" has become one of the most frequently used political slogans, next to "freedom" and "equality". As such, it stands together with these others in a certain suspicion of being used as an empty phrase,

D. Birnbacher (✉)
Heinrich-Heine-Universität Düsseldorf, Institut für Philosophie, Düsseldorf, Germany
e-mail: dieter.birnbacher@uni-duesseldorf.de

B. Schmitz-Luhn, C. Woopen (eds.), *Justice over the Course of Life*, Schriften zu Gesundheit und Gesellschaft - Studies on Health and Society 1,
https://doi.org/10.1007/978-3-030-86449-1_1

which can be filled with any contents for serving own interests and values. As there is no somehow binding and authoritative definition of social justice, there are barely any limits to the possibility of lamenting about all possible social inequalities—particularly if one is personally affected—as being "socially unjust" or "discriminative".

The most prominent among the social philosophers of the twentieth century, John Rawls, has the credit of having gone part of the way to mitigate the arbitrary nature of these interpretations. His main work *A Theory of Justice* (Rawls 1971) is the attempt to develop the core content of the idea of social justice as it is understood in present industrial societies and integrate it into a uniform and comprehensive concept of a fair society. It is disputed how far he has succeeded in this attempt and how far his theory brings together into a synthesis, the heterogeneous elements that are included in the concept of social justice. In view of its integrative nature, this theory nevertheless appears to be an appropriate starting point when it comes to questions of justice in social security institutions.

2 Social Justice à la Rawls

The basic idea of Rawls' conception of an integration of classic-liberal and social contents of the modern concept of social justice is that of a graduated hierarchy of principles related to a division of spheres: The core of the classic-liberal rights, which he calls "basic liberties", should unconditionally take priority over the other principles and simultaneously apply strictly universally. The claims that derive from these should be able to be possessed by any member of society, regardless of earnings, origin and other personal characteristics. According to Rawls—contrary to the liberal classicists and in addition to classic constitutional rights, such as freedom of religion and freedom of association—these "basic liberties" or "basic goods" also include self-respect, at least insofar as the possibility of respecting oneself depends on social factors.

While strict equality prevails on the first level, equal opportunities prevail on the second: Everyone should have the same opportunities to take on public offices. To what extent he actually takes these on depends on further—not equally distributable—factors, such as suitability and effort. Social justice even at this level does not coincide with equal results. In fact, various public functions are associated with different rights and duties and different positions of power. Social justice according to Rawls only requires that the opportunity to qualify for these offices exists in the same way for everyone.

It is only at the third level that aspects of *distributive justice* come into play with Rawls—on the one hand within the sphere of income, and on the other hand within the sphere of other natural inequalities or those resulting from social background. The distribution of income should only be able to be regarded as being socially fair insofar as the existing inequalities in the respective society are necessary to put the lowest earners into a better position over the longer term. According to Rawls, social justice also requires the compensation of all unequal life perspectives due to natural and social factors—insofar as they do not fall within the responsibility of the individual. The inequalities of naturally given circumstances, upbringing and social background, which are of crucial importance for the individual's opportunities in life should be compensated—within the bounds of efficiency of the society as a whole—as far as possible.

According to Rawls, such compensation is also necessary on the intergenerational level. The principle of the "fair savings rate" requires provision for future generations, at least insofar as those in the worst position of future generations are not put in a worse position than those in the worst position in the present generation, provided that this can be regarded as fair. Rawls' principle of intergenerational justice is a sustainability principle, with the particularity that he rejects any form of time discounting of future benefits and harms as being irreconcilable with justice. Benefits and harms that occur in the future must not be reduced ("discounted") in terms of their importance for the present merely for their futurity. As for the philosophers Epicurus, Spinoza, Kant and Schopenhauer, it is unjust for Rawls to undervalue the future consequences of present actions and omissions merely because they lie in the future. Future benefits and risks may only be discounted because of the extent that they are more uncertain.

More strongly than on the first and second level, the third level of Rawls' theory manifests a distinctly egalitarian tendency. Partly for that, it is also the most controversial level. What is particularly controversial is whether the people in the worst position, i.e. those with the lowest income/lowest opportunities in life, e.g. due to serious illness, disability or long-term unemployment, are entitled to the pronounced special position that Rawls assigns to them. The question is whether the extent to which the "difference principle", which summarises this orientation, can be reconciled with the predominant understanding of social justice. This principle requires to apply all economic and other social resources to the—possibly only minor—improvement of the fate of the poorest and most burdened, even if this means accepting that considerable deteriorations will take place in the economic and social living situation of all other persons, including those in a bad, but not in the worst position. Particularly for healthcare, it appears to follow from this that the healthcare services supplied by society must concentrate on those suffering the most hardship. It must provide them every benefit that relieves their fate even if this means that the healthcare services for all others have to be rigorously reduced (cf. Rauprich 2006, p. 72 f.).

This one-sidedness of Rawls' reconstruction of the concept of social justice can be overcome by assuming an alternative and intuitively more convincing principle, *weak prioritarianism*. This principle takes up the Rawlsian intuition that the idea of social justice primarily means improving the position of those who are relatively in the worst position, but does not limit the transfer of resources of the community of solidarity to the group of those in the worst position, but to the larger group of those in a below-normal position, depending on the extent to which they are in a worse position. Those in a relatively worse position are entitled to more extensive claims for solidarity benefits than others, as long as their opportunities in life are below the socially defined normal level, in accordance with the extent to which they are below this level.

Overall, the Rawlsian concept—disregarding the disputed "difference principle"—appears to be an appropriate basis for what can be looked upon as being socially fair in the area of social security:

1. The norms that universally and strictly apply to the system of social security are mainly those of safeguarding freedom, securing the minimum standard of living, which is expressed by the social minimum subsistence level and the assurance of the social bases of self-respect.
2. The second level of social justice with Rawls corresponds to the principle of equal access to social security, regardless of financial means, social standing and position of power. At this level, it no longer involves strict equality, but social equality of opportunities.
3. While social justice implies equal rights at the first and second level, at the third level, it implies a differentiation of justified claims according to the respective initial situation. As on the second level, it is based on a principle of solidarity. But beyond equal opportunities, it requires commitment to those who are particularly needy as a consequence of natural and social disadvantages, with the aim of an equalization of burdens.

3 Social Justice in Healthcare

Before I take a look at the existing old-age pension system in Germany on the basis of these principles, I will first briefly examine the healthcare system. Overall, the judgement appears appropriate that the existing healthcare system in Germany very largely satisfies the requirements of social justice in the Rawlsian sense.

With regard to the principle of safeguarding freedom, the patients' right to self-determination, which has been recently codified in law, protects the individual from being exposed to undesired medical paternalism. Except in emergency cases, mandatory treatment is only admissible if the patient's capacity for self-determination is either restricted temporarily or permanently or if the treatment is essential for protecting serious third-party interests. In recent years, a trend has developed away from paternalism by physicians in the Hippocratic tradition, and the wishes of patients have been taken more into consideration. However, considerable deficiencies still exist in respecting advance directives and in physician-patient communication. The *informed consent* of the patient for medical treatment, which has long been demanded in medical ethics, and the shared decision-making envisaged for the process of negotiating treatment targets and appropriate strategies continue to largely only exist on paper, not least because of the time pressure that prevails in many practices and hospitals.

The second level of social justice à la Rawls corresponds to the principle of equal access to healthcare services within the context of basic social services, regardless of financial means, social standing and position of power. Everyone has the same right to use healthcare services, but the general public is only obligated to offer (and perhaps advertise) this. Whether the offer is accepted remains the responsibility of the individual. There is no obligation to maintain health (cf. Patzig 1989) and it is not socially unjust if those who forego an offered healthcare service against their better judgement thereby suffer disadvantages.

The principle of equal opportunities is realized in the German system by giving the solidarity principle priority over the equivalence principle and by means of the system of statutory health insurance, to which approximately 90% of the population belongs and by which high-quality healthcare is provided for everyone regardless of financial status.

However, the German healthcare system does not fully satisfy the principle of equal opportunities, as a consequence of the historically grown juxtaposition of statutory health insurance funds based on the solidarity principle and private health insurance funds based on the equivalence principle. With approximately 10% of the insured persons, the share of private health insurance is higher than in any other EU country (with the exception of the Netherlands) (Rosenbrock and Gerlinger 2006, p. 117). Even under the (idealised) assumption that private patients receive the same treatment, due to this "two-class system", completely equal opportunities are out of the question. E.g. as physicians receive considerably higher fees for the same services with private patients than with statutory health insurance patients (in some cases many times the amount), a continuing incentive exists for them to give preference to private patients, e.g. with the allocation of appointments. In view of the considerable difference in fees, an average psychotherapist will give preference to private patients who are objectively less in need of treatment than statutory health insurance patients that are more in need of treatment, purely for reasons of survival. Equal opportunities are also compromised by the limitation of the insurance obligation in the statutory health insurance, the so-called assessment threshold. For insured persons with an income above this limit, it is generally more favourable to get insurance from a private health insurance scheme than pay the relatively higher premiums to the statutory health insurance fund. In individual cases, the better earners can virtually halve their premium rates in this way (Rosenbrock and Gerlinger 2006, p. 108 f.). On top of this, as private patients, they benefit from shorter waiting times, and in many cases also from a wider range of services.

It is no coincidence that these various inequalities are also reflected in the insured persons' subjective sense of justice. In a recent representative survey, 83.5% of Germans expressed a strong sense of injustice regarding the privileged treatment of people with private health insurance. Only 4.1% of all of those surveyed expressed only a minor sense of injustice. Interestingly, 10.4% of people in the group of those surveyed with a strong sense of injustice were people with private insurance (Braun and Marsted 2011, p. 3).

At the third level, solidarity obligations are added to this, which go beyond equal opportunities. Not only those in a worse health position as a result of disability, chronic illness, particular susceptibilities and age, but also due to poverty and social background, have an entitlement to welfare that goes beyond that of those in a better position, and this is not exhausted by the right to equal access.

There are also deficits in this respect. From relevant sociological studies it emerges that in Germany, not only the health condition of the group belonging to those who are socially the weakest is worst, but also that access to medical services is made more difficult for them by practice fees and pharmacy fees, which can become a noticeable financial burden for many low-earners. In several studies, it has been documented that burdens, inter alia, lead to insolvent persons avoiding going to a physician in case of illness (cf. Bioethik-Kommission Rheinland-Pfalz 2010, p. 58). It is also questionable whether the minimum health services presently granted to asylum-seekers and so-called sans-papiers in Germany satisfy the principle of specific solidarity obligations for those who are in the relatively worst position.

4 Social Justice in Old-Age Pension

With the question of social justice of the existing old-age pension system in Germany, the focus of the analysis shifts: For the old-age pension system other aspects of social justice and other aspects of the Rawlsian theory become relevant than those relevant for healthcare. The third level of the social and intergenerational equalisation of burdens moves into focus.

With regard to the first level, contrary to healthcare benefits, old-age pension benefits essentially involve financial benefits, and no *informed consent* is required for their acceptance. Neither do freedom of choice, such as the right to freely select physicians and insurance, play a role in pension insurance. However, the Rawlsian constitutional rights are relevant for old-age pension in at least four aspects:

1. From the principle of freedom the demand can be derived that every person insured in the social pension insurance scheme—analogously to the private healthcare by means of private supplemental health insurance—should have the freedom to additionally arrange for private pension provision, e.g. by means of private pension insurance or participation in a company old-age pension plan.
2. From the freedom principle it furthermore follows that everyone should have the freedom to continue pursuing employment above the pensionable age instead of receiving a pension. The reaching of pensionable age should not necessarily mean the end of employment. We are still far behind in this respect. Attempts at making the age limit more flexible have been made only tentatively. The limit should naturally not be opened up downwards so much that pension financing is put at risk due to a loss of contribution payments and an earlier start of pension benefit payments.
3. A factor that is of crucial importance for social justice in old-age pension provision is the assurance of the "social bases of self-respect", introduced as primary goods for the first time by Rawls in the core of the list of primary goods. This principle requires that the pension is not designed as alms of society, but as a legal entitlement. Those who have become unable to work as a consequence of age do not need to act as petitioners. They are not just entitled to the basic

security, but also to the old-age pension acquired as a result of their former employment, as something they have a right to.

Particularly this latter claim is fulfilled in the German pension system, so that it at least appears to have the character of insurance according to the equivalence principle. This appearance is strengthened by the fact that pension claims are differentiated on the basis of wages and therefore suggest that the individual receives, to a certain extent, what they paid into the pension fund. In several aspects, this does not correspond to reality. First of all, it is not the contributions that have been saved up by the pension recipients that determine the amount of the pension on the basis of the pay-as-you-go system, but the economic performance of the entirety of the employed cohorts. Secondly, the principle of so-called global equivalence has not been fulfilled for a long time, i.e. the contributions to the social security scheme have not been sufficient for pensions for a long time, so that these are increasingly being supplemented by the general tax revenue. Thirdly, similarly to the healthcare system, social redistribution takes place by the pension system. However, the illusion of assigning the amount of the pension to a self-ascribable "savings component" strengthens the appearance of having "earned" the pension and therefore furthers self-respect and a feeling of autonomy.

Undoubtedly, the principle of self-respect would be satisfied even better, if instead of trusting the pay-as-you-go system, everyone saved up for their old-age pension voluntarily and without governmental coercion. They could then ascribe their old-age pension to themselves with an even better intellectual conscience as own earnings and receive a feeling of self-respect from this. In addition to this, they would then be free from the paternalism due to the compulsory nature of insurance, where others determine their individual burden and the use of the saved funds. However, this possibility will remain utopian, as many are either not in a position or not free to voluntarily afford the required pension contribution payments. As a consequence of minimal working income, many would not be able to raise the necessary funds, while others would not want to. On the other hand, government coercion for voluntary pension would be paradox. The social compensation functions taken over from the statutory social security scheme would need to be based on different foundations in this case, such as those of general taxes. Higher earners would also need to bear (or insure) the risk of not being able to afford the pension contributions as a consequence of inability to work or unemployment.

At this point, the question arises of how compulsory insurance can be harmonised with the freedom principle, which, after all, is given priority by Rawls. With compulsory insurance for healthcare and old-age pension, is the social state not massively and unreasonably intervening in the personal freedom of deciding on the use of one's own income?

Interestingly, this question is barely ever asked, probably because the compulsory character of the necessary contributions to maintain the system is accepted without any problem in most industrialised countries. With healthcare and old-age-pension provision, only the amount of the contributions and the extent of the benefits covered by the solidarity system are disputed, particularly in view of the continuing rise in life expectancy and the increasing possibilities for medical intervention over time, most of which are more expensive than former ones.

On the basis of liberal values, the compulsory character of the social security systems requires justification in two aspects:

1. regarding the *solidarity* elements contained in both the statutory health insurance and in the pension insurance,
2. regarding the *paternalistic* elements contained in both the statutory health insurance and in the pension insurance.

The solidarity elements come less into conflict with social justice understood by Rawlsian principles than the paternalistic elements. In the Rawlsian concept of social fairness, there is no right to an income that is free from solidarity obligations. Solidarity financing is, in fact, the very core of the concept of a social state. What is more difficult to justify is the compulsory character of saving for later times. Can this kind of paternalistic compulsion be justified?

I think it can. One justification is the legitimate concern of the community of solidarity that, in the case of failing provisions for old age, they should not be required to pay for benefits that they cannot refuse in view of the principles of social justice. Another justification is the psychological fact that our capacity of realistically assessing our future requirements and of taking these adequately into account in present action is seriously limited. Two individually different yet universal trends generally lead to rationality deficits in this regard: pure time preference, the undervaluing of future benefits and losses for the sake of their futurity, and the "preference for present preferences" (cf. Birnbacher 1988, 31 f.) we do not presently share or understand or which we reject for moral, aesthetic or other reasons.

The social security schemes can therefore be regarded as a form of *external self-binding* through future-safeguarding institutions. Self-binding is always advisable if direct motivations are not sufficiently reliable to punctually fulfil acknowledged commitments. It limits the scope of future decision-making and actions through binding constraints and replaces direct motivation for long-term provisions by indirect motivation to keep unwanted short-term consequences of contract violations and terminations of agreements at bay. Anyone who knows that he tends to give in to opportunistic impulses (in accordance with Oscar Wilde's dictum from Lady Windermere's Fan, "I can resist everything except temptation"), but knows at the same time that he is putting his long-term goals into question, is generally well-advised to structure his decision-making options so that opportunistic motives tend to act in the "right" direction in the long term and tend to realise rather than thwart his overriding goals. External self-binding means, like Odysseus with the Sirens, using an external instance to limit one's own options and supporting self-discipline by external sanctions. If the background motivations are sufficiently rational, the implementation of the relevant external instance to prevent one's own (mis)conduct can be regarded as a type of *self-paternalism*: An external instance is made to limit one's own freedom of action for the benefit of one's own best interests. In contrast to external paternalism, self-paternalism does not pose any particular problem for the freedom principle. As the subject and object of the well-intentioned paternalism are the same person, the problem of limitation of autonomy does not apply, at least as long as the implementation of the external instance is fully voluntarily.

With regard to equality of opportunities, this principle stands and falls in old-age security with equality of opportunities on the labour market. In this respect, significant defects are increasingly being shown in many European countries from an intergenerational point of view, e.g. in high youth unemployment and increasing problems of younger people in starting a profession that corresponds to their skills, or even obtaining training to secure their opportunities on the labour market in the first place. The rate of youth unemployment in Spain already reached 50% in the mid-1990s (Vanhuysse 2013, p. 17). In many cases, right from the start, the training does not go in the direction that leads to skills that are appropriate for a relevant professional activity, due, inter alia, to a deterioration in the reputation of manual work in the widest sense. Therefore, the losses resulting from this for later old-age provision are not entirely due to a lack of equal opportunities, but also partially to unwise choices at a young age.

A series of serious and current problems arise in relation to old-age pensions regarding the third level of social justice according to Rawls, i.e. the principles of social equalisation of burdens and the principle of intergenerational justice.

In its present form, the German statutory pension insurance scheme comprises three components that aim at a redistribution of burdens in the sense of social equalisation:

1. In contrast to insurance according to the equivalence principle, the pension insurance scheme does not differentiate between groups with different life expectancy. In view of their shorter life expectancy, smokers, for example, are not charged less than non-smokers and men are not charged less than women, in spite of a significantly shorter life expectancy.
2. Additional factors of social equalisation in the sense of redistribution of the more efficient to the less efficient in terms of the prioritarianistic interpretation of the difference principle are the free co-insurance of family members, as well as the widows' and orphans' pensions.
3. In addition to this, in the calculation of pension entitlements, times during which no income has been earned or no contributions have been paid are also taken into consideration as insurance periods, among them maternity leave, unemployment, military service, illness and vocational training periods.

However, it remains an open question whether the German system of old-age pension is in its present form able to satisfy the Rawlsian requirements for intergenerational justice. The pay-as-you-go system entails that shrinking cohorts of employed persons due to demographic development must pay for the pension payments for a growing cohort of persons eligible for pensions. As in many other European countries, a continuing rise in life expectancy goes hand-in-hand with a falling fertility rate, so that in terms of numbers, the proportion between payers and recipients is becoming increasingly unfavourable.

The so-called Mackenroth Principle, according to which it does not ultimately matter whether pensions are financed by the pay-as-you-go method or the capital coverage method, no longer applies under the conditions of dramatic demographic change. According to the pay-as-you-go system that has been applicable in Germany since 1957, the professionally active generation finances the current statutory pension benefits that are payable with their contributions and taxes, insofar as these do not come from the pensioners themselves. With the capital coverage method, those who will later be pensioners save up the pension benefit payments themselves. However, deviations occur with a change in the numerical ratios. With the pay-as-you-go method, the pensions have the tendency of not corresponding to the development of the total economic performance of one's own generation, but rather that of the younger generations, so that the younger generation has much poorer prospects of reaching the amount of their parents' pensions if the relation between the numbers of payers and recipients continues to deteriorate. Those who will be disadvantaged are particularly women with short periods of employment. The risk cannot be dismissed that the pensions that the younger generation can expect will fall to a level that is difficult to reconcile with the Rawlsian sustainability principle that provision must be made so that the fulfilment of social justice can be ensured over the long term. As we have seen, this not only means that old-age provision ensures the social minimum subsistence level for everyone, but also that the pensions additionally satisfy the prioritarianistic principle of putting those in a relatively worse position into a better position and improving the large number of small pensions relative to the extent of approaching the social minimum subsistence level.

In Germany, steps have already been taken in order to make up for the generational imbalance in pension financing: One of these is the increase of the pensionable age. However, this is only reasonable to the extent that the working conditions are also improved for older people (the actual present average pensionable age is 59 to 63). This particularly requires that older people do not have the same burdens imposed on them as younger people and that they are protected more from health impairment as a result of work stress. The main source of psychological disorders in our society is psychological underchallenging and overburdening. Another step is taking account, in the pension calculation, of the demographic trend as well as of specific pension insurance contracts concluded with private insurance companies. Another step is government support for entering into additional private capital-covered pension insurance contracts. However, it is questionable whether these steps will be sufficient or whether much more extensive provisions would need to be formed in order to compensate the consequences of demographic shifts and improve the prospects of the next generation. Since money alone does not improve the position of future pensioners, the saved money must also be invested – a particular challenge in view of the presently prevailing disinclination to invest in Germany.

5 "Elderly Bias" in Social Policy?

In a democracy, there is inevitably a tendency to privilege groups that are of particular importance for elections and re-elections. An interesting case in this respect is the pension from the age of 63, which is particularly beneficial for long-term employed persons who are going to retire soon. It does not benefit the poorest, but rather parts of the population that can live relatively well on their pensions. On the other hand, it harms the younger generation by limiting their scope for making provisions against old-age poverty in the future.

There are many explanations as to why politicians primarily consider present elderly persons at the cost of those that will be elderly later. One is the dependency of the politicians on the goodwill of the relevant age group. On the one hand, the group that is positively affected amounts to a large number of people, while on the other hand, it is more politically "responsive" than any other. For example, participation in voting is the highest among people in their sixties and the lowest among young people. It is well known that, overall, citizens in the age group of around 60 participate more intensively in political life.

However, the trend towards "elderly spending" differs between countries. Studies show that the income of the generations born after 1955 is roughly equal to that of those born prior to this year in many countries. This applies to Scandinavia, for example, as well as to the English-speaking countries. However, according to sociologists Chauvel and Schröder, in France, Spain and Italy nearly all of the prosperity gains have been going to the generation born prior to 1960. According to these scientists, the explanation is excessive occupational protection for the old-established employees. "Anyone who joins the labour market during upturn phases will get a good job and will quickly be non-dismissible" (Chauvel and Schröder 2014, p. 31). The others are simply unlucky.

In the comparative study *Intergenerational Justice in Aging Societies* (Vanhuysse 2013), Pieter Vanhuysse investigated the ratio between government spending on the elderly (over 65) and government spending on younger people (under 25) in a number of industrialised countries in which the population is increasingly ageing, and developed an index that indicates to what extent a *bias* exists in favour of the elderly (*elderly-bias indicator of social spending*). Significant differences emerge between European countries with a comparable age structure. The index for Greece is 7 (i.e. the government spends 7 times more on the elderly than on young people), while Sweden's is 3.4. Other countries with a high index are Poland and Italy. With an index of 4.2, Germany is average. In total, 10 out of 29 OECD countries spend more than five times as much on every elderly person than on every younger person.

One of the instruments that Pieter Vanhuysse recommends in order to ensure a fair share of public spending on the younger generations is the introduction of *proxy voting* by parents for their children who are not yet eligible to vote. In this way, the rights of the upcoming generation might be strengthened—of course, under the (possibly unrealistic) condition that parents cast the additional vote in the interest of securing the future of their children. This proposal—along with its difficulties—

has been under discussion for quite a time (cf. Van Parijs 1998). Among the proposals for strengthening the vested interests of young people against the "elderly bias" of politicians, it seems one of the most attractive.

References

Bioethik-Kommission Rheinland-Pfalz. 2010. *Gesundheit und Gerechtigkeit. Ethische, soziale und rechtliche Herausforderungen [Health and justice. Ethical, social and legal challenges]*. Mainz: Ministerium der Justiz.

Birnbacher, D. 1988. *Verantwortung für zukünftige Generationen [Responsibility for future generations]*. Stuttgart: Reclam.

Braun, B., and G. Marsted. 2011. Vertrauen und Gerechtigkeit – (wie) beeinflussen sie Einstellungen und Verhaltensweisen im Gesundheitswesen? [Trust and justice – (how) do they affect attitudes and behaviour in public health care?] *Gesundheitsmonitor* 1: 1–5.

Chauvel, L., and M. Schröder. 2014. Die verlorene Generation. Südeuropas Jugend wird abgehängt [The lost generation. The youth of Southern Europe gets outpaced]. *DIE ZEIT* 25 12.06.2014: 31.

Patzig, G. 1989. Gibt es eine Gesundheitspflicht? [Is there an obligation for health?] *Ethik in der Medizin* 1: 3–12.

Rauprich, O. 2006. Gleiche Gesundheit und soziale Gerechtigkeit [Equal health and social justice]. In *Gerecht behandelt? Rationierung und Priorisierung im Gesundheitswesen [Justly treated? Economisation and prioritisation in public health]*, eds. B. Schöne-Seifert, A. M. Buyx, and J. S. Ach, 51–87. Paderborn: Mentis.

Rawls, J. 1971. *A theory of justice*. Cambridge, MA: Belknap Press.

Rosenbrock, R., and T. Gerlinger. 2006. *Gesundheitspolitik. Eine systematische Einführung [Health policy. A systematic introduction]*. 2nd ed. Bern: Huber.

Van Parijs, P. 1998. The disenfranchisement of the elderly, and other attempts to secure intergenerational justice. *Philosophy and Public Affairs* 27: 292–333.

Vanhuysse, P. 2013. *Intergenerational Justice in Aging Societies. A cross-national comparison of 29 OECD countries.* Gütersloh: Bertelsmann-Stiftung.

Who Cares for What? Determinants of Preparation for Old Age Across the Life Course

Klaus Rothermund

Dear Professor Woopen, dear Ladies and Gentlemen,

I want to begin by expressing my heart-felt thanks for being invited to this wonderful symposium. When Professor Woopen called me a few weeks ago and asked whether I'd be willing to give a lecture on fairness across the life course, my initial reaction was: "Why me?" This feeling increased while I was listening to Prof. Di Fabio's lecture. No one likes to be the next speaker following such a brilliant talk. Furthermore, I have to confess that justice and fairness are not at the top of my research agenda. I am an empirical psychologist. I collect and evaluate data. My colleagues and I show only little interest in how these statistics relate to justice and fairness. Indeed, among psychologists, it's considered good form to leave normative questions aside altogether. But my doubts vanished when Frau Woopen told me, "Mr. Rothermund, just give your lecture and present your results. The audience and I will take care of thinking about how this relates to issues of fairness." I was relieved. Accordingly, the words "fairness" or "justice" do not occur again in my lecture. Instead I will present a few of my findings and rely on the audience to draw its own conclusions about how they pertain to fairness.

So, what is my lecture about if not fairness? My subject is preparation for old age. Among German residents, this may bring to mind the Riester pension scheme. This isn't a bad start for a first association, but while retirement plans like the Riester scheme are part of old-age preparation, financial issues are clearly not everything (Lang and Rohr 2013). In reality, old-age preparation is a very complex, multi-layered phenomenon. It comprises preparation for all possible changes that one expects in the course of getting older. What types of old-age preparation do we need and how do we think about the expected changes?

K. Rothermund (✉)
Institute of Psychology, University of Jena, Jena, Germany
e-mail: klaus.rothermund@uni-jena.de

B. Schmitz-Luhn, C. Woopen (eds.), *Justice over the Course of Life*, Schriften zu Gesundheit und Gesellschaft - Studies on Health and Society 1,
https://doi.org/10.1007/978-3-030-86449-1_2

Why is old-age preparation an interesting topic not only for individuals but also for society as a whole? The answer is: shifting demographics. What does this mean? In the past few decades, life expectancy has increased dramatically, and the trend is likely to continue. People are living longer and longer. But increased life expectancy does not benefit every phase of life equally. The extra years we get are—"unfortunately," some might say—tacked on at the end. In other words, our increased life expectancy primarily extends the phase that we call "old age", and that phase has become drastically longer. Those who retire at 60, 65 or 67 often have a quarter of their lives still ahead of them—a quarter that aging individuals must prepare for and plan.

From a political and societal standpoint, increased life expectancy brings with it a different problem. Coupled with a chronically low birth rate, it creates a disproportion between contributors and receivers in social security systems. Fewer people pay into the system, and more people take, and they take for longer periods. It is to be expected—or to be feared—that at some point provision bottlenecks will occur, making it impossible to finance the levels of retirement insurance, health insurance, and nursing care insurance to which we are currently accustomed.

It is no wonder that politicians think about and sometimes call for restricting state retirement pensions because they can no longer be financed. Out of concern that people could be left penniless in old age, they have begun to demand that persons prepare early on and assume responsibility for their own retirement.

I believe that this is a politically legitimate demand that we as a society must come to terms with. Politicians tend to think: I decide and the people will have to follow suit eventually because they have to. But what they ignore, or at least neglect, is the question of how individuals process this demand and the imminent changes it reflects. How have people responded to the demand that they should be responsible for their own old age? Has it made its way into their heads? Which new motivations and attitudes have emerged as a result? What are favorable and unfavorable frameworks for implementing such a demand?

If we look at current research, we won't find many answers to these questions. There are studies that describe the extent of financial planning or health behavior. But we still lack a systematic approach to psychological factors, motivations, and attitudes towards how we organize our lives. My colleagues and I created the research project "Aging as Future" to fill the gaps in our knowledge (Universität Jena 2015). Generously funded by the Volkswagen Foundation as part of its program Key Questions in Science and Society, this interdisciplinary project is staffed by psychologists, sociologists, and psychogerontologists. It examines people's attitudes about organizing their lives in old age as well as the psychological factors and societal circumstances that influence how people prepare for old age. Through our partners in the United States and in Hong Kong we are also investigating the influence of different cultures of aging on how individuals age. Unfortunately, data collection in the United States and in Hong Kong is still ongoing and I have no conclusions to the present day. Instead I want to present some fascinating preliminary data from our German panel study (Kornadt and Rothermund 2011a, 2011b, 2012, 2014, 2015; Kornadt et al. 2013; Rothermund 2014).

The first question we asked ourselves is what is old-age preparation, and how can one measure it? We carried out a pilot study and asked people of varying ages about the changes they expect to come with old age, their attitudes towards old age, what they are doing specifically to prepare for it. One thing became apparent right away: preparation for old age is a complex, multidimensional phenomenon. It is based on specific functions and areas of life. There is not *one* form of old-age preparation, for which one does a lot or a little. People expect very different and very specific problems and changes to occur during the process of aging, and the extent of old-age preparation in one area is independent of old-age preparation in others. The most essential part of old-age preparation is the prevention of health problems. Another area is preparation for changes at the workplace. How can I make sure that I can adapt to changing professional requirements as long as possible?

This last question may become more interesting after profession-based age limits in Germany are loosened (Rothermund 2014): How can I ensure that I am competitive in older age and can still be employable? Leisure time is also an important subject for old-age preparation. In old age we have more freedoms because many time-consuming obligations drop out, and this free time must be planned (Ekerdt and Koss 2016, Münch 2014). What are suitable leisure activities in old age? Which will be practical in older age, and which will I still be able to enjoy? What can I do so I can do these activities in old-age well?

Another increasingly important subject is how we deal with emergencies and exceptional situations. What about power of attorney and health care proxies? When should a will be written? These are questions that affect all of us at some point (Lang and Wagner 2007). Housing for seniors is another interesting subject. How do I want to live after I retire? Where do I want to live? What kind of amenities do I need? Perhaps I want to live close to my family. I also want to remain physically and mentally fit. How will I look? People start raising these questions around the age of 50. Do I have enough money for life after I retire? Can I take care of myself without being a burden to others? Do I have money left over to support children, grandchildren or other close persons financially? (See Rager et al. 2012)

The pilot project interviews showed that if we want to measure and collect data on old-age provision, we have to be specific. Here is an example from the survey that we developed for this purpose (see Fig. 1).

We have identified nine domains of life in which we measured how individuals have prepared for old age. For each area, we asked three questions: To what extent am I taking measures to prepare for this domain? How much thought have I given this topic? To what extent have I informed myself and talked to others about this topic? For each of these nine domains, we quantified preparation by merging the results from the three questions. In taking our measurements, we decided elected not to record specific activities. In some areas there are many different things that one can do or not do to prepare oneself for old age. It would be very difficult to list all these activities and ask about each one. The bigger problem, however, is that the motivation for why a person carries out an activity is often unclear. One can, say, diet to prevent health problems in old age—but also to lose weight and look better right now. In examining old-age preparation, it is important to measure the quantity and

1. Financial situation in old age	not at all	a little	quite a bit	a lot
I am actively providing for my financial situation in old age (e.g. retirement accounts, savings, etc.)	❑	❑	❑	❑
I think about the topic.	❑	❑	❑	❑
I try to gather information about the subject and discuss it with others.	❑	❑	❑	❑

2. Occurrence of emergency situations in old age (need for nursing care, death, dementia)	not at all	a little	quite a bit	a lot
I am actively preparing for the occurrence of emergency situations (e.g. testament, patient's provision, health care proxy, etc.).	❑	❑	❑	❑
I think about the topic.	❑	❑	❑	❑
I try to gather information about the subject and discuss it with others.	❑	❑	❑	❑

3. Mental and physical fitness in old age	not at all	a little	quite a bit	a lot
I am actively working to maintain my mental and physical fitness in old age (e.g. by physical activity, athletics, regular mental activity etc.).	❑	❑	❑	❑
I think about the topic.	❑	❑	❑	❑
I try to gather information about the subject and discuss it with others.	❑	❑	❑	❑

Fig. 1 Questionnaire to assess levels of domain-specific preparation for old age (sample domains: finances, emergencies, fitness)

intensity of activities performed specifically with the goal of improving life in old age. Our surveying method takes into account this functional differentiation (Kornadt and Rothermund 2014). We handed out these surveys to 800 persons equally distributed between the ages of 30 and 80 (Kornadt and Rothermund 2011a). The same respondents completed the survey in 2009 and 2014, so we could record changing attitudes towards old-age preparation over time.

Let's look at the results. Here is a chart showing age trends for domain-specific old-age preparation (Fig. 2; see also Kornadt and Rothermund 2014).

At first glance, the table looks complicated. But it can be understood quite simply. Each line stands for a domain in which one can prepare for old age. Let us first look at the younger people from our survey. There are generally two types of preparation. The first includes the standard forms: savings, fitness, and health. Here younger people have gotten the message that they need to prepare early on. They indicate that

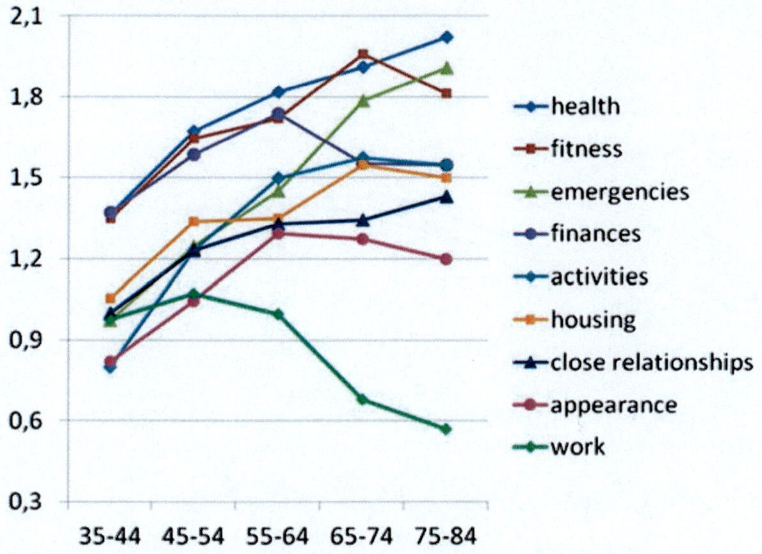

Fig. 2 Age trends in domain-specific preparation for old age

they are already doing quite a bit in these domains. The other cluster of domains covers emergencies, activities, housing, close relationships, appearance, and work. Here the amount of preparation young people undertake is relatively low.

The older one gets, the more the preparation people take in each domain varies in interesting ways. Health remains a favorite. It becomes more and more important and remains the domain with the highest preparation. Preparation for physical and mental fitness also remains at a high level. This is the only domain that occasionally rises above health in importance. The biggest increase over the life course goes to preparation for emergencies. The biggest decrease goes to preparation for work. This is no big surprise in Germany, where very rigid retirement age limits regulate the labor market. By the age of 55 or 60, it no longer makes sense to invest in one's professional career, because there is very little possibility for putting one's new experience and knowledge to use. Younger people we surveyed had a different attitude to professional preparation for old age, showing considerably higher values than the 55 and over group. This may indicate that younger people are already counting on being professionally active in older age—whether because they have to or because they are permitted to or because they can.

We have here a fairly complex picture of the different forms of old-age preparation and the way they change with increasing age. I now want to simplify the material somewhat and place the different forms of preparation into two overarching categories (Kornadt and Rothermund 2014). First, we can identify preparation for what Peter Laslett (1989) termed "The Third Age". This age begins generally with retirement and covers the period in which we are still active and engaged, want to enjoy life, and can still plan old age constructively. Preparation for the third age consists of the domains activities/leisure, friends, close relationships, work, fitness,

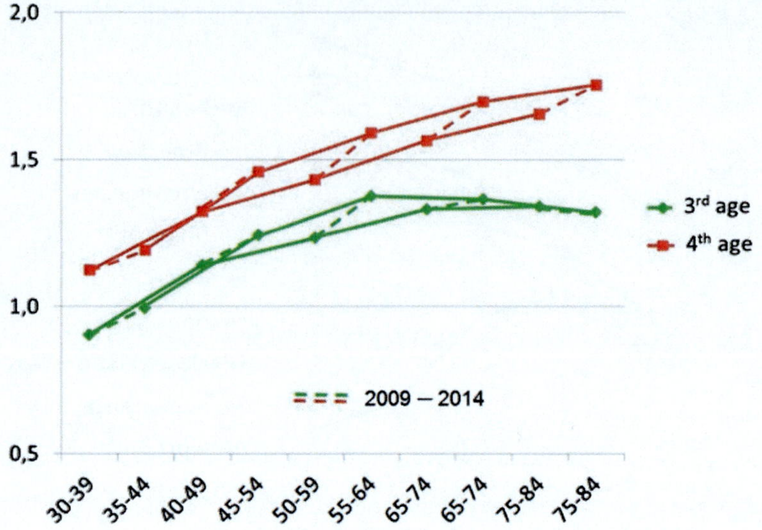

Fig. 3 Longitudinal changes in preparation for the third and fourth age for different age groups

and appearance. The other category is primarily about preparation for what Paul Baltes (1997) calls "The Fourth Age". It consists of preparations for difficulties and emergencies associated with very old age, for a time when one is in need of care and dependent on others.

Looking at these two broad categories, we can discern a pattern. Preparation for the fourth age—when we may no longer be autonomous—gets more attention than preparation for the third age. This seems only logical. Everyone does it, and they do a lot of it. The form of preparation increases linearly over the age range in our survey. The older one grows, the more important this form of preparation becomes, and the more measures are taken. Preparation for the third age increases with age, too, but reaches its zenith between 60 and 65, and then remains relatively high but does not increase any further.

The next figure (Fig. 3) contains another interesting finding. The longitudinal aspect of our study shows changes over a 5-year interval. For all age groups we found a marked increase in preparation intensity. Interestingly, this upturn cannot be explained by the increasing age of participants alone. The increase in preparation intensity over the five-year interval is generally stronger than the differences between age groups. That is, the increase in preparation between 2009 and 2014 is steeper than the age increases between the neighboring cohorts. What does this increase mean? It would appear that over the past five years old-age preparation has generally gained in importance for all age groups in our survey.

In Germany, the topic of old-age preparation has indeed moved to the fore. People from all age groups think more about preparing for retirement and have become more active. This historical increase directly concerns preparation for the dependent, fourth age. This may reflect decreasing trust in the viability of the state pension system. The emphasis on increased long-term care and nursing costs in the media and reports about the horrifying conditions in some old-age homes appear to have fostered individual preparation for the fourth age across all age groups. But preparation for the third age has drastically increased as well, though its extent very much depends on age. Until around the age of 65, we see a considerable rise; above that, preparation intensity remains the same, and even drops off a bit. A possible explanation for this stagnation is that the extent of preparation depends not only on perceived need and the desire for an active life in old age, but also on energy and time. But these resources decrease in old age. Active forms of preparing for and living in old age reach their limits, giving way to forms of living that emphasize acceptance and values (Brandtstädter and Rothermund 2002; Brandtstädter et al. 2010; Rothermund and Brandtstädter 2003a).

Let us take stock of the trends we have identified so far. Preparing for old age is a topic that affects us all. We have found that, with the exception of certain domains and age groups, preparation intensity for the fourth, dependent age is generally stronger than for the third, independent age. We also found an increase in preparation for the third and the fourth ages across all demographic groups over the past five years.

In the second part of my lecture, I want to focus on differences among individuals. People do not prepare for old age to the same degree, even within the same demographic group. Which variables determine these differences? To find out, we looked at various groups of predictors. First there are the social factors such as age, sex, and net income. We also looked at the societal framework. How do people see opportunities for participation in social life? Which possibilities exist for older people? What is health care provision like for older people? How do older people see it? We then examined the individual construction of age and aging resulting out of these factors. What are people's attitudes towards living in old age as an individual person? Do they look forward to it or do they see it as a threat? Do they have specific plans and goals for old age or is that a phase of life that they would rather not think about?

I have tried to structure the results of our analysis clearly and I will present them incrementally without assuming any background knowledge in psychology or methodology. Unfortunately, I can't spare you from more diagrams and figures. I will look at the separate determinants for the prediction of differences in old-age preparation for the third and fourth ages. In doing so, I will also point out some interesting differences we found between age groups (see Kornadt and Rothermund 2014; Kornadt et al. 2015).

Let us start with socio-structural variables (Fig. 4a). We already know that age is one of the main determinants of preparation. The older one gets, the more preparations one makes. This is illustrated in the positive vectors that extend from age to preparation. As I already noted, this type of age dependence is stronger with regard to fourth age preparation than for third age preparation. Generally, women report having made more preparations than men. Household net income also plays a certain role, but only when preparing for the fourth age. Income does not have an effect on preparation for the third age once age or sex have been controlled.

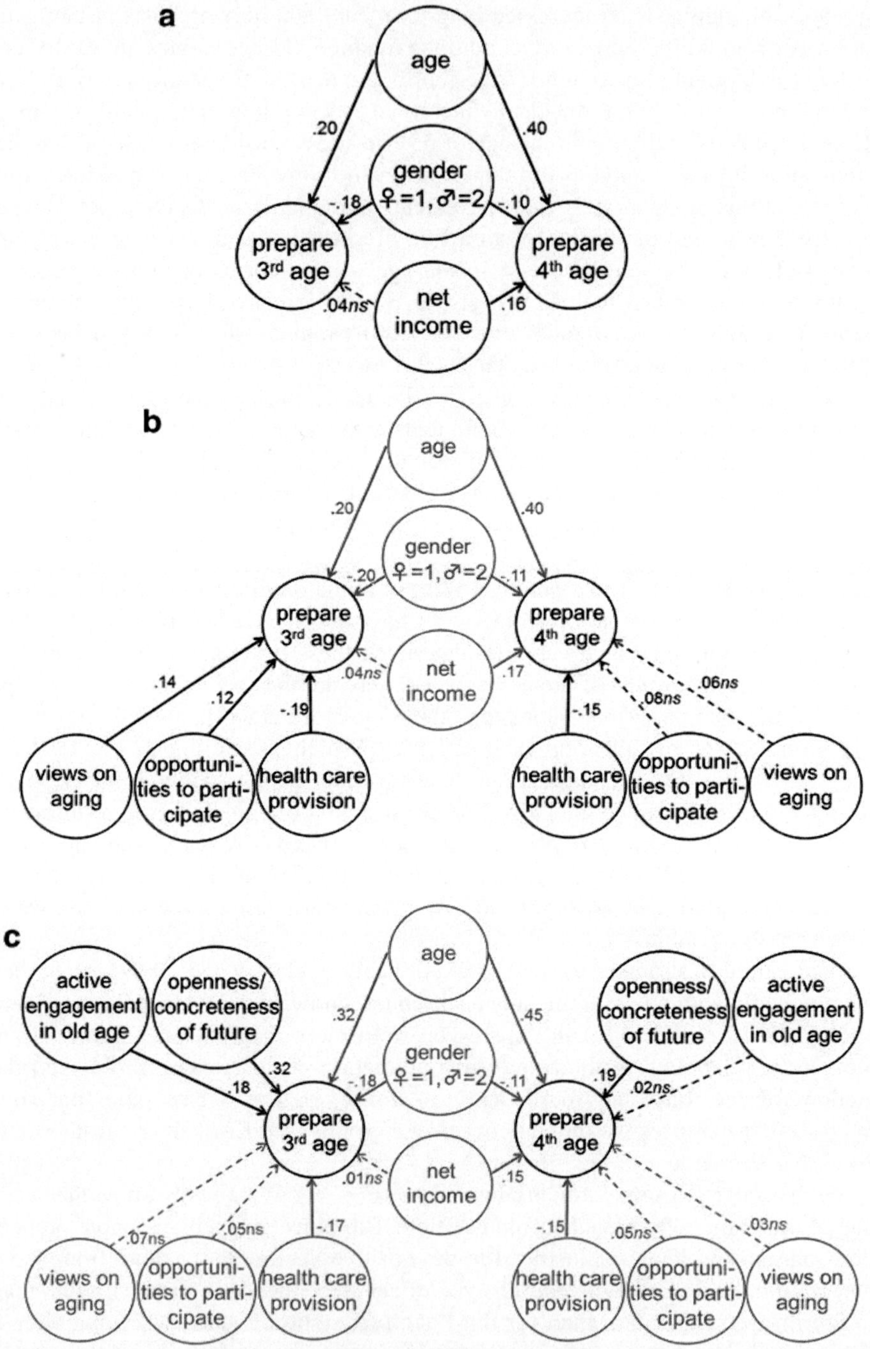

Fig. 4 (**a**) Determinants of preparation for old age: Socio-structural variables. (**b**) Determinants of preparation for old age: Societal variables. (**c**) Determinants of preparation for old age: Individual constructions of aging

Let's turn to the societal variables now (Fig. 4b). An interesting variable concerns beliefs about health care provision in old age. How do people see health care provision in age and how do differing attitudes affect old-age preparation? Today's media regularly emphasize that people cannot count on receiving sufficient pensions from the state. State pensions are already inadequate and we should assume that state pensions will see further cuts in the future. We find that people who expect health care provision in old age to be bad or to worsen, prepare more. The negative representations thus seem to have had an effect (cf. Lang et al. 2013). A little bit of fear is, after all, a proven means to get people to act. The negative path from health care provision to preparation for the fourth and third ages indicates that individual preparation increases when fear of poor health care provision in old age increases. This is a form of psychological compensation (Baltes and Baltes 1990; Rothermund and Brandtstädter 2003b). People try to offset expected deficits by making more preparations.

Interestingly, we observe positive effects for the other two predictor variables: A person who assesses the situation of older people in society as positive prepares *more* for his or her own old age. Those who believe that older people receive respect and recognition, and who see possibilities for meaningful participation in old age, devote more planning to retirement. In other words, assessing this phase of life as worthwhile, as offering possibilities for being involved in society without being relegated to the old-age home, is a prerequisite for taking the helm and preparing one's retirement. Provided, that is, that the phase of life concerned is the third age. The same is true for the opposite case. People who have a negative view of old age and have internalized negative old-age stereotypes (Kornadt and Rothermund 2011, 2012; Rothermund 2005; Rothermund and Brandtstädter 2003a) make *fewer* preparations for old age (Kornadt et al. 2015). It appears, then, that the prospect of an active and meaningful old age is a central motivation for preparing one's retirement with foresight. By contrast, negative stereotypes, fixed retirement ages, experiences with marginalization, and restricted possibilities of meaningful participation in social life adversely affect motivation for old-age preparation.

Now, in a final step, let us turn to specific individual constructions of aging and attitudes towards planning one's old age. These variables are the direct motivational determinants of individual action (see Fishbein and Ajzen 1975; Lang and Carstensen 2002; Zimbardo and Boyd 1999). They are the best predictors of how we prepare for old age (Fig. 4c). In our study we measured two parameters: One scale assesses the openness of an individual's future time perspective (Brandtstädter and Rothermund 2003; Brandtstädter et al. 1997): How often and specifically do I think of my life in old age? Do I have specific goals and plans for my life in old age that I want to achieve? Do I see meaningful activities for myself? Envisioning an open and purposeful future generally has a positive effect on how individuals prepare for retirement, especially with regard to the third age. The absence of a clear future time perspective, whether because of a restricted life horizon (Rothermund and Brandtstädter 1998) or because of insufficient possibilities for organizing retirement and participating in social life, presents a serious obstacle for individual preparation for old age.

We also developed a scale that measures attitudes towards active life planning in old age (Kornadt and Rothermund 2011b). Based on this scale we collected data on people's willingness to lead an active and fulfilling life in old age and employ their personal skills and experiences. A positive attitude towards such active and task-centered life organization in old age has a positive effect on preparation for the third age, but not on preparation for the fourth age.

In addition to these direct effects of time perspective and age-related attitudes towards old-age preparation, there is another interesting connection. In this final figure (Fig. 4c) we see that as soon as these proximal determinants are plugged into the model, the effects of the societal factors disappear. This means that the effects of how we perceive our old age and our societal participation in old age are communicated via such motivational factors and attitudes toward planning one's life in old age. Someone who has a positive view of old age tends to have specific plans for a more active life when they are old. Accordingly, they also prepare more for old age.

Let me now summarize my central findings. When it comes to the fourth age, preparation for old age is important and widespread. This is a universal, or normative, form of age-related activity. With few exceptions everyone does what they can, even younger people, and the older they get the more they do. There are some other factors that influence preparation, but these are mostly negative. In particular, the belief that state benefits for things like health care and nursing will dwindle increases compensatory measures in individual preparation.

Preparation for the third age, however, shows large differences among individuals, and for this reason it is probably more politically and societally significant. Several factors play an important role in individual old-age preparation for this age: positive views of old age and the possibilities for participation in old age. If people see viable options for living their lives in old age and experience older people as an important and valuable part of society, they are ready and motivated to plan their old age and prepare accordingly. These effects—products of the societal framework—are conveyed through specific attitudes and goals that a person has for their old age. Only when we understand old age as a phase of life that we can shape, and not as a fear-ridden, worthless, despised, and marginalized period of life, are people motivated and willing to prepare for their later years.

I can sum up my lecture in three short statements. First, we must remember that old-age preparation is not only about money and health. Our study has shown that old-age preparation is a complex phenomenon spanning very different areas of life. And for each age-related change there is an equivalent form of preparation. Second, negative views of old age and participation options after retirement make old age seem undignified and inhibit active preparation and planning. Third, political demands for individual responsibility for old age also bring with them political obligations. Those who demand such responsibility must also create conditions that encourage individual preparation and active participation in older age. Society must ensure that old age is seen as a worthwhile phase of life, that age limitations are dismantled and that age discrimination is eliminated (Rothermund and Mayer 2009; Rothermund and Temming 2010). Only if something really substantial changes in the social reality of life in old age a new idea of old age can take hold in people's heads. By breaking down barriers, creating flexible options for older people to participate in society, and considering their interests and desires in the areas of work, culture, housing, and recreation, society can produce a positive vision of aging. Old age must be a phase of life that people look forward to, there must be possibilities for meaningful activity, the elderly must not be removed from society and marginalized. As long as we don't secure these structural and motivational underpinnings, we cannot demand that individuals take more responsibility for old age (Rothermund 2014).

In conclusion I would like to thank everyone who assisted with the project "Aging as Future", in particular Anna Kornadt, Peggy Voss, Stephan Lessenich, and Frieder Lang. I also want to thank the Volkswagen Foundation for its generous funding. I hope you've enjoyed my talk and I thank you for your kind attention.

References

Baltes, P. B. 1997. Die unvollendete Architektur der menschlichen Ontogenese: Implikationen für die Zukunft des vierten Lebensalters [The incomplete architecture of human ontogeny: Implications for the future of the fourth age]. *Psychologische Rundschau* 48: 191–210.

Baltes, P. B., and M. M. Baltes. 1990. Psychological perspectives on successful aging: The model of selective optimization with compensation. In *Successful aging: Perspectives from the behavioral sciences,* eds. P. B. Baltes and M. M. Baltes, 1–34. Cambridge, MA: Cambridge University Press.

Brandtstadter, J., and K. Rothermund. 2002. The life-course dynamics of goal pursuit and goal adjustment. A two-process framework. *Developmental Review* 22: 117–150.

Brandtstädter, J., and K. Rothermund. 2003. Intentionality and time in human development and aging: Compensation and goal adjustment in changing developmental contexts. In *Understanding human development: Dialogues with life-span psychology,* eds. U. M. Staudinger and U. Lindenberger, 103–124. Dordrecht: Kluwer.

Brandtstädter, J., K. Rothermund, D. Kranz, and W. Kühn. 2010. Final decentrations: Personal goals, rationality perspectives, and the awareness of life's finitude. *European Psychologist* 15: 152–163.

Brandtstädter, J., D. Wentura, and U. Schmitz. 1997. Veränderungen der Zeit- und Zukunftsperspektive im Übergang zum höheren Alter: Quer- und längsschnittliche Befunde [Changes of the perspective on time and future in transition to higher age: Cross-sectional and longitudinal findings]. *Zeitschrift für Psychologie* 205: 377–395.

Ekerdt, D. J., and C. Koss. 2016. The task of time in retirement. *Ageing and Society* 36: 1295–1311.

Fishbein, M., and I. Ajzen. 1975. *Belief, attitude, intention and behavior: An introduction to theory and research.* Reading, MA: Addison-Wesley.

Kornadt, A. E., and K. Rothermund. 2011a. Contexts of aging: Assessing evaluative age stereotypes in different life domains. *Journal of Gerontology: Psychological Sciences* 66: 547–556.

Kornadt, A. E., and K. Rothermund. 2011b. Dimensionen und Deutungsmuster des Alterns – Vorstellungen vom Altern, Altsein und der Lebensgestaltung im Alter [Dimensions and interpretative patterns of aging: attitudes about aging, being old and ways of living in old age]. *Zeitschrift für Gerontologie und Geriatrie* 44: 291–298.

Kornadt, A. E., and K. Rothermund. 2012. Internalization of age stereotypes into the self-concept via future self-views: A general model and domain-specific differences. *Psychology and Aging* 27: 164–172.

Kornadt, A. E., and K. Rothermund. 2014. Preparation for old age in different life domains: Dimensions and age differences. *International Journal of Behavioral Development* 38: 228–238.

Kornadt, A. E., and K. Rothermund. 2015. Views on aging: Domain-specific approaches and implications for developmental regulation. *Annual Review of Gerontology and Geriatrics* 35: 121–144.

Kornadt, A. E., P. Voss, and K. Rothermund. 2013. Multiple standards of aging: Gender-specific age stereotypes in different life domains. *European Journal of Ageing* 10: 335–344.

Kornadt, A. E., P. Voss, and K. Rothermund. 2015. Hope for the best – prepare for the worst? Future self-views and preparation for age-related changes.

Lang, F. R., and L. L. Carstensen. 2002. Time counts: Future time perspective, goals, and social relationships. *Psychology and Aging* 17: 125–139.

Lang, F. R., D. Weiss, D. Gerstorf, and G. G. Wagner. 2013. Forecasting life satisfaction across adulthood: Benefits of seeing a dark future? *Psychology and Aging* 28: 249–261.

Lang, F. R., and M. K. Rohr. 2013. Eigennutz und Gemeinsinn: Altersvorsorge ist mehr als die Sorge ums Geld [Self-interest and public spirit: Old-age provision is more than worrying about money]. In *Verbrauchervielfalt. Chancen des demographischen Wandels für Konsum und Finanzen [Consumer diversity. Opportunities of demographic change in consumption and finance]*, ed. M. Freytag, 232–241. Frankfurt: FAZ.

Lang, F. R., and G. G. Wagner. 2007. Patientenverfügungen in Deutschland: Bedingungen für ihre Verbreitung und Gründe der Ablehnung [Living will incidence in non-clinical population samples: Conditions and reasons for refusal]. *Deutsche Medizinische Wochenschrift* 132: 2558–2562.

Laslett, P. 1989. *A fresh map of life: The emergence of the third age*. London: Weidenfeld and Nicholson.

Rager, B., F. R. Lang, and G. G. Wagner. 2012. Sparmotive von jungen, mittelalten und älteren Erwachsenen – Erste Ergebnisse eines neuen Inventars zur Erfassung lebenslaufbezogener Sparmotive [Motives for saving of young, middle-age and older adults – First results of a new inventory for the recording of saving motives over the course of life]. *Zeitschrift für Gerontologie und Geriatrie*. 45: 742–747. doi:10.1007/s00391-012-0322-6.

Rothermund, K. 2005. Effects of age stereotypes on self-views and adaptation. In *The adaptive self: Personal continuity and intentional self-development,* eds. W. Greve, K. Rothermund, and D. Wentura, 223–242. Göttingen: Hogrefe and Huber.

Rothermund, K. 2014. Die Gestaltung des Alters. Ein Plädoyer für mehr Psychologie [Shaping age. A plea for more psychology]. *Psychologische Rundschau* 65: 95–99.

Rothermund, K., and J. Brandtstädter. 1998. Auswirkungen von Belastungen und Verlusten auf die Lebensqualität: alters- und lebenszeitgebundene Moderationseffekte [Effects of burdens and losses on the quality of life: Moderating effects tied to age and lifetime]. *Zeitschrift für Klinische Psychologie* 27: 86–92.

Rothermund, K., and J. Brandtstädter. 2003a. Age stereotypes and self-views in later life: Evaluating rival assumptions. *International Journal of Behavioral Development* 27: 549–554.

Rothermund, K., and J. Brandtstädter. 2003b. Coping with deficits and losses in later life: From compensatory action to accommodation. *Psychology and Aging* 18: 896–905.

Rothermund, K., and A.-K. Mayer. 2009. *Altersdiskriminierung – Erscheinungsformen, Erklärungen und Interventionsansätze [Age discrimination – Manifestations, explanations and approaches to intervention]*. Stuttgart: Kohlhammer.

Rothermund, K., and F. Temming. 2010. *Diskriminierung aufgrund des Alters [Discrimination on the grounds of age]*. Berlin: Antidiskriminierungsstelle des Bundes.

Universität Jena. 2015. Altern als Zukunft [Ageing as Future]. http://www.alternalszukunft.uni-jena.de/. Accessed June 28, 2021.

Zimbardo, P. G., and J. N. Boyd. 1999. Putting time in perspective: A valid, reliable individual-differences metric. *Journal of Personality and Social Psychology* 77: 1271–1288.

Age Categories in Social Security Systems

Stefan Huster

1 Age Limits Under the Law

1.1 Aging and the Law

People moving through various stages of life will continue to be a fact of human existence for the foreseeable future: we are born, passing through childhood and adolescence; then we become adults, pursuing career and family goals; and finally, we arrive at old age, enjoying our golden years in tranquility. It would be very difficult to imagine our lives unfolding in any other way.

The law accommodates this basic fact of life and typically contains specific rules for minors, adults and the elderly. In this sense, every modern body of laws presupposes age categories, such as those governing the right to vote, to enter into contracts, to receive pension benefits, as well as those determining when the mandatory school age begins and ends—and much else. Age categories are therefore ubiquitous throughout the legal system.[1] This fact alone makes it seem rather unlikely that such categories could be problematic from a normative standpoint.

And yet, throughout various eras, societies and cultures, these life stages have varied greatly in content and duration. Law itself has contributed to this fact: to

[1] Cf. Magdalena Pöschl, Altersdiskriminierung und Verfassung, in: Studiengesellschaft für Wirtschaft und Recht (pub.), Alter und Recht, 2012, pp. 47, 55 ff. See also: die Bestandaufnahme bei Peter Häberle, Altern und Alter des Menschen als Verfassungsproblem, in: FS Lerche, 1993, pp. 189 ff.; and then Gerhard Igl, Altersgrenzen als altersspezifisches Regelungsinstrument, in: Ulrich Becker/Markus Roth (ed.), Recht der Älteren, 2103, pp. 165 ff.

S. Huster (✉)
Ruhr Universität Bochum, Lehrstuhl für Öffentliches Recht, Sozial- und Gesundheitsrecht und Rechtsphilosophie, Bochum, Germany
e-mail: stefan.huster@rub.de

B. Schmitz-Luhn, C. Woopen (eds.), *Justice over the Course of Life*, Schriften zu Gesundheit und Gesellschaft - Studies on Health and Society 1,
https://doi.org/10.1007/978-3-030-86449-1_3

mention only the most obvious example, this happened when statutory pension insurance was introduced, turning elderly people into retirees.[2] So, while the law is influenced by the aging process, our very understanding of that process is, in turn, also influenced by the law.[3]

1.2 Age Categories: Clarity and Arbitrariness

We now come to a second observation. As long as there exists a functioning system for registering people, age categories will have a significant practical advantage: they are clear and easy to determine by looking at a personal ID, which makes them hard to tamper with and therefore ideally suited to legal use—especially when administering large numbers of people. However, this advantage of simplicity, which gives them an egalitarian character to be explained later in more detail,[4] is also at the same time a disadvantage: they ignore any distinction between individuals and treat all members of a given age group exactly alike. This is especially apparent when an age limit is used as a proxy for some other characteristic, or is at any rate justified as an associated characteristic—such as when a person is forced to give up a profession at a certain age on the grounds that they would normally no longer possess sufficient capacity to perform the job. Some individuals will naturally prove the exception to the rule. A similar—and inevitable—arbitrariness characterizes the related legal custom of the deadline: being denied a more favorable consequence under the law by missing a deadline by one day, or perhaps even by just a few hours, can be frustrating or even tragic for an individual, but time limits must be imposed at some point.

1.3 Justice Among Generations and Age Cohorts

We now come to a third and final observation: age categories are criticized for two different reasons that are not always properly distinguished.[5] This can clearly be seen in controversies involving the age of retirement. Some argue that the newly introduced "retire at 63" rule will disadvantage the younger generations now having

---

[2]Cf. Christoph Conrad, Vom Greis zum Rentner, 1994.

[3]Cf. Bericht der Sachverständigenkommission, Sechster Bericht zur Lage der älteren Generation in der Bundesrepublik Deutschland: Altersbilder in der Gesellschaft, 2010, pp. 373 ff.; Stefan Ruppert/Kathrin Brunozzi/Christian Lange, Zur Entstehung des heutigen Standardlebenslaufs aus rechtshistorischer Sicht – zugleich ein Beitrag zu den juristischen Implikationen des demographischen Wandels, RW 2012, pp. 77 ff.; and articles in: Lebensalter und Recht. Zur Segmentierung des menschlichen Lebenslaufs durch rechtliche Regelungen seit 1750, Stefan Ruppert (ed.), 2010.

[4]See below at Sect. 2.3.

[5]For more on this distinction, see below at Sect. 2.3.

to finance this tax-subsidized early-retirement assistance scheme [*Lebensleistungsrente*], even though, owing to demographic trends, they have no hope of ever receiving such a benefit themselves.[6] This objection raises the issue of intergenerational fairness (or more precisely, birth cohort fairness) regarding cost/benefit sharing.

The situation, however, looks very different when age limits are criticized for being overly rigid, or—in the case of certain (usually latter) stages of life—even implicitly derogatory devices which may fail to determine accurately the relationship between various life phases. Consider, for example, fixed age limits for practicing a profession which make no exceptions for individual circumstance or capacity. This is where the accusation of "age discrimination" comes into play.[7] Such an accusation is based on demographic trends only in the actual sense that age discrimination against older people becomes more noticeable the older they get and the more numerous they are. This, though, has nothing to do with relations between various birth cohorts—except, of course, in the trivial sense that age limits always affect specific individuals who belong to different cohorts; but such is the case with every legal policy generally, not just those involving intergenerational justice. Moreover, laws against age discrimination also protect younger people.[8]

2 Are Age Limits Discriminatory?

2.1 Trends and Debates in Constitutional and European Law

In legal arguments, the laws of the European Union have now become the strongest weapon against age limits. Framework directive 2000/78/EC was enacted based on Art. 13 EC (cf. Art. 10 and 19 of the Treaty on the Functioning of the European Union); it is well known that both legal documents address age discrimination.[9] Art. 21 Sec. 1 of the Charter of Fundamental Rights of the European Union also provides for an explicit ban on age discrimination, which is made even more forceful in the case of the elderly by a special law recognizing and respecting it in Art. 25 of the

[6]For more information on the equal-protection aspect, cf. Stefan Huster/Andrea Kießling, Gesetzgebung im Sozialstaat und gleichheitsrechtliche Dogmatik. Irrungen und Wirrungen am Beispiel der "Rente mit 63", ZRP 2014, pp. 171 ff.

[7]See for example: Susanne Baer, Demografischer Wandel und Generationengerechtigkeit, VVDStRL 68 (2009), pp. 290, 338 ff.

[8]In practice relevant, e.g., to the hitherto common policy of giving older workers more vacation-time (cf. BAGE 141, 73 ff.) or the age-graduated pay scales of civil servants (most recently, see i.a. EuGH v. 19.6.2014, C-501/12, NVwZ 2014, pp. 1294 ff.).

[9]For more on this, see, e.g., Christian Hartig, Altersdiskriminierung im öffentlichen Dienst, 2014; Martin Lüderitz, Altersdiskriminierung durch Altersgrenzen, 2006; Felipe Temming, Altersdiskriminierung im Arbeitsleben, 2008.

charter.[10] Granted, Art. 13 EC was merely an authorization provision[11] and the framework directive has just as little relation to the social security systems of member states as the Charter of Fundamental Rights does. Nevertheless, there are quite a few provisions in EU law allowing us to infer that distinctions relating to age are especially problematic with respect to the notion of equality under the law. In principle then, it is hardly surprising that, against this backdrop, the European Court of Justice (ECJ) has now inferred a ban on age discrimination from the concept of equal treatment.[12]

The German constitution contains no such ban. The Federal Constitutional Court has so far either not addressed the question of age limits from an equal-treatment standpoint, or has been very reticent on the subject. However, in constitutional law debates in Germany—which often follow trends in European law—one now notices that age-related distinctions are also being increasingly judged critically, and that the Federal Constitutional Court is being urged in this regard to assume a noticeably stricter supervisory role in the area of equality before the law generally.[13]

2.2 *Reservations Concerning a General Ban on "Age Discrimination"*

A first glance at national constitutional debates will reveal misgivings on the subject of fundamentally intensifying the judicial review of age limits from an equal-protection standpoint. Ever since the Constitutional Court abandoned a pure doctrine of arbitrariness, the differentiation between person-related and case-related distinctions has played a central role in defining evaluation criteria in cases involving equal protection—a role which was in essence already being debated under the

[10] For more, see, e.g., Ching-Hui Chen, Die speziellen Diskriminierungsverbote der Charta der Grundrechte der Europäischen Union. Eine Strukturanalyse unter besonderer Berücksichtigung des Verbots der Altersdiskriminierung, 2011.

[11] Cf. only Odendahl, in: Heselhaus/Nowak (eds.), Handbuch der Europäischen Grundrechte, 2006, § 43 Rn. 44 with further references.

[12] ECJ, Rs. C-144/04 (Mangold), Slg 2005, I-9981. Cf. also Huster, Gleichheit im Mehrebenensystem: Die Gleichheitsrechte der Europäischen Union in systematischer und kompetenzrechtlicher Hinsicht, EuR 2010, pp. 325, 334 ff. with further references.

[13] Cf. especially Susanne Baer, Demografischer Wandel und Generationengerechtigkeit, VVDStRL 68 (2009), pp. 290, 338 ff.; Ssoufian Bouchouaf, Statistische Altersdiskriminierung, KJ 2006, pp. 310, 315 ff.; Doris König, Das Verbot der Altersdiskrminierung – ein Diskriminierungsverbot zweiter Klasse?, in: FS Zuleeg, 2005, pp. 341, 356 ff.; ead., Handlungsbedarf bei der Umsetzung des Altersdiskriminierungsverbots?, ZESAR 2005, pp. 218, 222 f.; Thomas Mann, Gesetzliche Höchstaltersgrenzen und Verfassungsrecht, in: FS Starck, 2007, pp. 319, 327 ff.; Angelika Nußberger, Altersgrenzen als Problem des Verfassungsrechts, JZ 2002, pp. 524, 530 ff.; Siros Simitis, Altersdiskriminierung – die verdrängte Benachteiligung, NJW 2094, pp. 1453 f.; Peter J. Tettinger, Rechtsprechungslinien des Bundesverfassungsgerichts zu Höchstaltersgrenzen als berufsbezogenen Regelungen, DVBl. 2005, pp. 1397, 1402 ff.

Constitution of the Weimar Republic,[14] along with all other problems of demarcation. It follows from this that unequal treatment for reasons relating to one's person should be subject to a strict proportionality test (whatever that may mean from an equal-protection standpoint[15]), while fact-based reasons would still be sufficient for making distinctions merely relating to the case.[16]

Now age appears at first glance to be just such a person-related characteristic: it is a property that a person cannot change of their own volition. And precisely this fact might lead us to favor a strict legal test and, correspondingly, a basic attitude of "suspicion" towards age limits. On closer inspection, however, this will not do. In the opinion of the Federal Constitutional Court, it is those very same distinguishing characteristics that approximate the discrimination characteristics described in Art. 3 Sec. 3 of the Constitution which they see as especially problematic, making them similar to sex, race, national origin and religion.[17] These characteristics are distinguished by the fact that they define fixed and to a large extent enduring categories of people who, experience has shown, are also particularly susceptible to prejudice or discrimination. This, however, is *not* true of age: we all grow older and are therefore affected by age limits in the same way.[18] One initiative against age limits succinctly (and with unintended humor) demonstrated the point with the following paradoxical slogan: "Age discrimination is a form of discrimination that we all face." One could only respond by saying: If everyone is affected by it, then it cannot be discrimination.[19]

Those who hold German law to be deficient for lack of a general ban on age discrimination[20] would do well to consider the fact that the US Supreme Court has also rejected such a ban on similar grounds. The high court refused to classify age as a presumptive basis for discrimination under the equal-protection clause of the US Constitution, stating: "Older persons have not been subjected to a history of purposeful and unequal treatment [...] Old age also does not define a discrete and insular minority because all persons, if they live out their normal life, will experience

[14] Cf. the articles of E. Kaufmann and H. Nawiasky, Die Gleichheit vor dem Gesetz im Sinne des Art. 109 der Reichsverfassung, VVDStRL 3 (1927), pp. 2 ff., 25 ff.

[15] For a critical treatment, see: Stefan Huster, Rechte und Ziele, 1993, pp. 164 ff.

[16] For a description of the case-law history see: Uwe Kischel, in: Volker Epping/Christian Hillgruber (ed.), Grundgesetz, 2. Aufl. 2013, At. 3 Rn. 24 ff.

[17] Cf. BVerfGE p. 88, p. 87, pp. 96 f.

[18] Cf. also Magdalena Pöschl, Altersdiskriminierung und Verfassung, in: Studiengesellschaft für Wirtschaft und Recht (eds.), Alter und Recht, 2012, pp. 47, 55 ff.; ead., Gleichheit vor dem Gesetz, 2008, pp. 494 ff., 711 ff.

[19] Naturally, this phenomenon is also not unknown to scholars of ethical philosophy; cf. Thomas Nagel, Equality and Partiality, 1991, p. 69: "Remember that the subject of an egalitarian principle is not the distribution of particular rewards to individuals at some time, but the prospective quality of their lives as a whole, from birth to death." This topic was also treated in Dennis McKerlie's book, Justice Between the Young and the Old, PPA 30 (2002), pp. 152 ff.

[20] For an example of this line of thought, see: Thomas Mann, Gesetzliche Höchstaltersgrenzen und Verfassungsrecht, in: FS Starck, 2007, pp. 319, 327.

it [...] Age is not a suspect classification under the Equal Protection Clause".[21] Likewise, under German law there is little basis for considering age in general as a proscribed reason for making distinctions between persons.[22]

It is indeed noteworthy and surprising that the EU member states have accepted a ban on age discrimination at the European level, when their own national constitutions still do not include such strict bans.[23] In the light of what was discussed earlier, it is easy to see why. This does not mean that connections between age and the discrimination against persons of a *certain* age—in the job market, for example—cannot become problematic. And so we find that many member states themselves have provisions for combating age discrimination in specialized areas. EU and national regulations on age discrimination also deal primarily with the subjects of work and employment.

The zeal for laws imposing a general ban on age discrimination at the EU-level should be seen less as an attempt to find appropriate solutions to the problem, and more as an effort to compensate for the member states' own deficiencies on the issue. It has since become apparent that such commitments simply cannot be kept. Relevant directives, Germany's General Law of Equality and the ECJ's case law all admit of numerous exceptions to the ban on age discrimination when dealing with subject of age limits.[24]

2.3 *The Egalitarian Character of Age Limits*

Age limits can have not only a good regulatory purpose, but even a peculiarly egalitarian character—a character inextricably linked to the concept of justice, as they in a certain sense treat all alike and without regard to individual particularities.

There are some age limits that everyone will assent to: those required for voting or holding elective office, for example, are essential to the democratic system; any case-by-case handling of the right to make political choices would undermine its egalitarian essence. In another yet similar way, age limits are bound up with the concept of justice when they mandate retirement at a certain age, so as to give the younger generation a chance. Here we can easily see how absurd it would be to criticize such

[21] Kimel et. al. v. Florida Board of Regents, 528 U.S. pp. 62, 83 (2000).

[22] Once again see: Pöschl, Altersdiskriminierung und Verfassung, in: Studiengesellschaft für Wirtschaft und Recht (ed.), Alter und Recht, 2012, pp. 47 ff. Cf. also ead., Gleichheit vor dem Gesetz, 2008, pp. 494 ff., 711 ff.

[23] The lone exception would appear to be Art. 6. Para. 2 of the Constitution of Finnland—a country whose influence on European legal trends has not been especially pronounced up to now.

[24] For a recent overview of the subject, see: Bernd Schulte, Altersgrenzen im Arbeits- und Sozialrecht und gesellschaftliche Teilhabe aus rechtlicher Sicht, ZFSH/SGB 2014, pp. 395, 400 ff. For a somewhat more favorable assessment of these exceptions made on the basis of the special nature of the age criterion, consult Ulrich Becker, Die alternde Gesellschaft – Recht im Wandel, JZ 2004, pp. 929, 935.

rules as age discrimination: someone who retires from being a college professor at 65 or 67 will only have acquired the position to begin with because their predecessor retired at some point, too. Consequently, such rules are also generally accepted by existing case law.

In German legal and political debates, age limits in matters related to healthcare are widely considered taboo; while in the field of medical ethics, the question as to whether age can be considered a legitimate criterion for prioritizing the allocation of scarce medical resources is the subject of much debate.[25] One could object right away that this should be a matter of biological rather than chronological age. But precisely on the basis of this contradistinction, it can be shown that the connection with chronological age can have a very egalitarian basis.

Germany's Transplantation Act requires that organs be distributed based on relative urgency and prospects for success (cf. § 12 Para. 3 S. 1 Transplantation Act). These are both defensible prioritization criteria whose relationship to one another is, however, notoriously problematic: while urgency constitutes the original criterion of fairness that takes into account individual need, the prospects for success are a results/benefit-oriented criterion whose utilitarian nature can become cause for concern. How would we handle a case where the potential organ recipients do not differ with respect to urgency or prospects for success, but are of different ages? If, say, a very ill 25-year-old and a hale and hearty 80-year-old both need the same organ for transplant, it is hardly clear that the question of the age difference should play no role at all. Even if the 80-year-old were in better health and would enjoy a longer remaining life expectancy with the organ, one could still see it as a special form of urgency and priority for the younger but worse-off patient, since he is already in need of a new organ at such a young age while his competitor has already lived a normal lifespan. If one had to choose between living five more years as the 25-year-old, versus living another ten as the 80-year-old—without having the slightest idea as to the actual state of one's own health—it might not be unreasonable to choose the former option, even if the case for it were not completely unimpeachable. And if such a choice is conceivable from an individual perspective, there is no reason why it should be considered out of the question when creating a system of collective distribution from the beginning.[26] But here we can also see in what sense

[25] For more on this debate and what follows, see: Stefan Huster, Sozialstaat oder soziale Gerechtigkeit? Zum Spannungsverhältnis von politischer Philosophie und Verfassungsrecht am Beispiel der Altersrationierung im Gesundheitssystem, in: Robert Alexy (ed.), Juristische Grundlagenforschung (ARSP-Beiheft Nr. 104), Stuttgart (Franz Steiner) 2005, pp. 202–217; id., Altersrationierung im Gesundheitswesen: (Un-)Zulässigkeit und Ausgestaltung, MedR 2010, pp. 369–372; id., Alter als Priorisierungskriterium, in: Björn Schmitz-Luhn/André Bohmeier (eds.), Priorisierung in der Medizin. Kriterien im Dialog, Berlin/Heidelberg (Springer), 2013, pp. 215–223, each with further references. For a more comprehensive treatment of the subject from a legal perspective, see: Christian Held, Das Alter als zulässiges Rationierungskriterium in der Gesetzlichen Krankenversicherung?, 2011.

[26] This evidently follows Norman Daniels' line of thought: Daniels, Just Health Care, 1985, pp. 86 ff.; id., Am I My Parent's Keeper? 1988; id., Justice and Justification, 1996, Part II; id., Justice between the Young and the Old, in: Walters (ed.), Choosing Who's to Live, 1996, pp. 24 ff.

the linkage with chronological rather than biological age has an egalitarian character: Chronological age, we now understand, allocates the chances of acquiring an organ in the course of one's life equally, while taking into account biological age—and the same is true of considering the prospects of success—privileges those who are still in comparatively good health. Biological age represents in this case the criterion of utility, as it would lead us to decide against rendering medical treatment to the person in worse health in favor of overall utility maximization; in contrast, linking the decision to chronological age would in a certain sense be guided much more strongly by the ideal of equal treatment.

Whether or not one is willing to consider age limits when apportioning health care resources depends, in the first case, on whether one believes that limitations on service are necessary at all. Those who believe that untenable cost increases in healthcare can be avoided with other measures—even in light of the current demographic trends in many modern societies and advances in medical technology—will not be inclined to go in the direction of rationing according to age. But it could be the case that this assumption is not realistic—and precisely *because* of the development of cost-intensive treatments that lengthen life spans. If at this point we now decide that cost savings are necessary, would it be completely unreasonable to ascribe a higher priority to lengthening the life of a 25-year-old than that of an 80-year-old? Would it not be fairer to apportion scarce resources along these lines?

Of course, the age criterion will never become a key prioritization criterion in real-life healthcare systems. But the simple refusal to ponder age limits at all cannot be justified by considerations of equity. On the contrary: it should again be emphasized that age-as-prioritization-criterion is extremely unsuited to resolving problems involving intergenerational justice (or more precisely: cohort justice)[27] and demographic trends. The fact that certain illnesses are especially common and therefore increase healthcare expenses is *per se* no reason to limit treatment options for such conditions, any more than the growing percentage of older people is a reason to cut spending on their particular age group. The reverse is just as true: Age as a criterion of prioritization is a subject worthy of discussion regardless of what gives rise to the need for rationing. What we call intergenerational justice—i.e. the equitable distribution of costs and benefits among various birth cohorts—is a true interpersonal distribution problem, since one's own birth cohort can never be changed; rather, one ages with it. In contrast, the rational distribution of costs and benefits at different stages of a person's life is, first and foremost, merely an *intra*-personal problem, because all of us will pass through these stages of life. Thus, entirely different criteria are needed here.

[27] For more on this distinction, see above at Sect. 1.3.

3 Conclusion

Age limits can be problematic for the law, but not necessarily. Connecting them with other forms of discrimination—sex, race, creed, etc.—is almost always wrong; unlike these, using age as a deciding factor is usually defensible. A comprehensive ban on age discrimination that would render all age limits fundamentally illegitimate without an especially strict equal-treatment test would therefore not be constructive. This is ultimately a function of the fact that questionable age limits are unwise rather than unjust: We all suffer—individually as well as socially—if, for example, the mandatory retirement age is too inflexible. That, however, is not a case of unfair or discriminatory treatment of a certain group, but rather an example of unwise social and economic policy. And so the age limit for panel physicians was abolished as soon as it became clear that there was a shortage of them.[28]

Developments of this sort are likely to occur ever more frequently as the population continues to age. This, though, will be primarily a consequence of social demand rather than of the individual rights of those who wish to continue working. A discrimination ban would misinterpret these issues—which arise out of demographic trends and changing notions of age for organizing society—as issues of distribution. But they are not. Therefore, what we need is not a general ban on age discrimination, but rather case specific rules for dealing sensibly with matters involving age.

References

Baer, S and W. Kluth. 2009. Demografischer Wandel und Generationengerechtigkeit [Demographic change and intergenerational equity]. *Erosion von Verfassungsvoraussetzungen. Veröffentlichungen der Vereinigung der Deutschen Staatsrechtslehrer* 68: 246-380.

Becker, U. 2004. Die alternde Gesellschaft – Recht im Wandel [The Aging Society – Law in Transition]. *JuristenZeitung* 59 (19): 929-938.

Bericht der Sachverständigenkommission an das Bundesministerium für Familie, Senioren, Frauen und Jugend. 2010. *Sechster Bericht zur Lage der älteren Generation in der Bundesrepublik Deutschland. Altersbilder in der Gesellschaft [Sixth status report on the Federal Republic of Germany's senior generation. Images of age in society].* Berlin: BMFSFJ.

Bouchouaf, S. 2006. Statistische Altersdiskriminierung – ein Problemaufriss anhand von Beispielen aus der Rechtsprechung des Bundesverfassungsgerichts [Statistical age discrimination – outlining the problem on the basis of examples taken from the Federal Constitutional Court's jurisdiction]. *Kritische Justiz* 3: 310-319.

Chen, C. 2011. *Die speziellen Diskriminierungsverbote der Charta der Grundrechte der Europäischen Union. Eine Strukturanalyse unter besonderer Berücksichtigung des Verbotes der Altersdiskriminierung [Specifics of nondiscrimination rule of the European Union's Charter of Fundamental Rights. A structural analysis with special consideration of the prohibition of age discrimination].* Baden-Baden: Nomos.

[28] For more on this, see Jacob Joussen, in: Ulrich Becker/Thorsten Kingreen (eds.), SGB V, 4. A. 2014, § 95 Rn. 27 f. Zur Verfassungsmäßigkeit der Altersgrenze von 68 Jahren für die Kassenzulassung vgl. BVerfG NJW 1998, pp. 1176 ff.

Conrad, C. 1994. *Vom Greis zum Rentner. Der Strukturwandel des Alters in Deutschland zwischen 1830 und 1930 [From old man to retiree. Structural change of old age in Germany between 1830 and 1930]*. Göttingen: Vandenhoeck & Ruprecht.

Daniels, N. 1985. *Just Health Care*. Cambridge: Cambridge University Press.

Daniels, N. 1988. *Am I My Parent's Keeper?: An Essay on Justice Between the Young and the Old*. Oxford: Oxford University Press.

Daniels, N. 1996a. *Justice and Justification. Reflective Equilibrium in Theory and Practice*. Cambridge: Cambridge University Press.

Daniels, N. 1996b. Justice between the Young and the Old. In *Choosing Who's to Live: Ethics and Aging*, ed. J. W. Walters, 24-46. Champaign: University of Illinois Press.

Häberle, P. 1993. Altern und Alter des Menschen als Verfassungsproblem [Aging and old age as a constitutional problem]. In *Wege und Verfahren des Verfassungslebens. Festschrift für Peter Lerche zum 65. Geburtstag*, eds. P. Badura, R. Scholz, 189-212. München: C.H. Beck.

Hartig, C. 2014. *Altersdiskriminierung im öffentlichen Dienst [Age discrimination in the public sector]*. Berlin: Duncker & Humblot.

Held, C. 2011. *Das Alter als zulässiges Rationierungskriterium in der Gesetzlichen Krankenversicherung?[Age as a permissible rationing criterion in statutory health insurance?]* Hamburg: Verlag Dr. Kovač.

Huster, S. 1993. *Rechte und Ziele. Zur Dogmatik des allgemeinen Gleichheitssatzes [Rights and objectives. Dogmatics in the general principle of equality]*. Berlin: Duncker & Humblot.

Huster, S. 2005. Sozialstaat oder soziale Gerechtigkeit? Zum Spannungsverhältnis von politischer Philosophie und Verfassungsrecht am Beispiel der Altersrationierung im Gesundheitssystem [Welfare state or social justice? The tension between political philosophy and constitutional law, using the example of age rationing in health care systems]. In *Juristische Grundlagenforschung. Tagung der Deutschen Sektion der Internationalen Vereinigung für Rechts- und Sozialphilosophie vom 23.-25. September 2004 in Kiel*. ed. R. Alexy, 202-217. Stuttgart: Franz Steiner Verlag.

Huster, S. 2010a. Altersrationierung im Gesundheitswesen: (Un-)Zulässigkeit und Ausgestaltung [Age rationing in health care systems: (In)Admissibility and design]. *Medizinrecht* 28 (6): 369-372.

Huster, S. 2010b. Gleichheit im Mehrebenensystem: Die Gleichheitsrechte der Europäischen Union in systematischer und kompetenzrechtlicher Hinsicht [Equality in multi-level systems: Considering the European Union's equality rights in systematic and competence-related terms]. *Europarecht EuR* 45 (3): 325-337.

Huster, S. 2013. Alter als Priorisierungskriterium [Age as priority criterion]. In *Priorisierung in der Medizin. Kriterien im Dialog [Prioritization in medicine. Criteria in dialog]*, eds. B. Schmitz-Luhn, A. Bohmeier, 215-223. Berlin/Heidelberg: Springer Verlag.

Huster, S. and A. Kießling. 2014. Gesetzgebung im Sozialstaat und gleichheitsrechtliche Dogmatik. Irrungen und Wirrungen am Beispiel der "Rente mit 63" [Welfare state legislation and dogma of equality. Aberrations and confusions using the example of the 'pension at 63']. *Zeitschrift für Rechtspolitik* 47 (6): 171-174.

Igl, G. 2013. Altersgrenzen als altersspezifisches Regelungsinstrument [Age limits as an age-specific regulatory instrument]. In *Recht der Älteren [Rights of the elderly]*, eds. U. Becker, M. Roth, 165-191, Berlin, Boston: Walter de Gruyter.

Joussen, J. 2014. Commentary of §§ 24i, 44–51, 95–98, 317 SGB V. In *SGB V, Gesetzliche Krankenversicherung. Kommentar [Public health insurance. Commentary]*, eds. U. Becker, T. Kingreen. München: C. H. Beck.

Kaufmann, E. and H. Nawiasky. 1927. *Die Gleichheit vor dem Gesetz im Sinne des Art. 109 der Reichsverfassung: Der Einfluss des Steuerrechts auf die Begriffsbildung des öffentlichen Rechts: Berichte [Equality before the law in the sense of Article 109 of the Reich Constitution: How tax law influenced the concept formation in public law: Reports]*. Berlin: Walter de Gruyter.

Kischel, U. 2013. Commentary on At. 3 Rn. In *Grundgesetz GG*, eds. V. Epping, C. Hillgruber, München: C. H. Beck Verlag. pp. 124 et seq.

König, D. 2005a. Das Verbot der Altersdiskriminierung – ein Diskriminierungsverbot zweiter Klasse? [Prohibition of age discrimination – a second-class discrimination ban?] In *Europa und seine Verfassung. Festschrift für Manfred Zuleeg zum siebzigsten Geburtstag [Europe and its constitution. Festschrifts in honor of Manfred Zuleeg's 70th birthday]*, eds. C. Gaitanides, S. Kadelbach, G. C. R. Iglesias, 341-361. Baden-Baden: Nomos.

König, D. 2005b. Handlungsbedarf bei der Umsetzung des Altersdiskriminierungsverbots? [Need for action in implementing the prohibition of age discrimination?] *Zeitschrift für europäisches Sozial- und Arbeitsrecht, ZESAR* 4 (5/6): 218-224.

Lüderitz, M. 2006. *Altersdiskriminierung durch Altersgrenzen. Auswirkungen der Antidiskriminierungsrichtlinie 2000/78/EG auf das deutsche Arbeitsrecht [Age discrimination through age limits. Effects of the Anti-Discrimination Directive 2000/78/EC on German Labor Law]*. Bern: Peter Lang.

Mann, T. 2007. Gesetzliche Höchstaltersgrenzen und Verfassungsrecht – Ansätze zu einer verfassungsrechtlichen Neubestimmung [Legal age limits and constitutional law – Approaching redefinitions of legal age limits in constititutional law]. In *Die Ordnung der Freiheit: Festschrift für Christian Starck zum siebzigsten Geburtstag [The Order of Freedom: Festschrift for Christian Starck on his 70th Birthday]*, eds. R. Grote, I. Härtel, K.-E. Hain, T. I. Schmidt, T. Schmitz, G. Folke Schuppert, C. Winterhoff, C. Starck, 319-334. Tübingen: Mohr Siebeck.

McKerlie, D. 2002. *Justice Between the Young and the Old*. Oxford: Oxford University Press.

Nagel, T. 1991. *Equality and Partiality*. Oxford: Oxford University Press.

Nußberger, A. 2002. Altersgrenzen als Problem des Verfassungsrechts [Age limits as a problem of constitutional law]. *JuristenZeitung* 57 (11): 524-532.

Odendahl, K. 2006. § 43, Rn. 44. In *Handbuch der Europäischen Grundrechte [Manual of European Fundamental Rights]*, eds. S. Heselhaus, C. Nowak, München: C. H. Beck Verlag.

Pechstein, M. 2014. Commentary on EuGH, 19.06.2014 - C-501/12, C-502/12, C-503/12, C-504/12, C-505/12, C-506/12, C-540/12, C-541/12: Altersdiskriminierung für Beamtenbesoldung [Age discrimination for civil servants' salaries]. *Neue Zeitschrift für Verwaltungsrecht* 19: 1294–1301.

Pöschl, M. 2008. *Gleichheit vor dem Gesetz [Equality before the law]*. Wien, New York: Springer.

Pöschl, M. 2012. Altersdiskriminierung und Verfassung [Age discrimination and the Constitution]. In *Alter und Recht [Age and law]*, ed. Studiengesellschaft für Wirtschaft und Recht, 47-70. Wien: Linde Verlag.

Ruppert, S., K. Brunozzi, and C. Lange. 2012. Zur Entstehung des heutigen Standardlebenslaufs aus rechtshistorischer Sicht – zugleich ein Beitrag zu den juristischen Implikationen des demographischen Wandels [Considering the origin of today's standard curriculum vitae from a legal-historical perspective – A contribution to the legal implications of demographic change]. *Rechtswissenschaft* 3 (1): 77-110.

Ruppert, Stefan. 2010. *Lebensalter und Recht. Zur Segmentierung des menschlichen Lebenslaufs durch rechtliche Regelungen seit 1750 [Age and law. Segmentation of the human life course through legal regulations since 1750]*. Frankfurt am Main: Verlag Vittorio Klostermann.

Schulte, B. 2014. Altersgrenzen im Arbeits- und Sozialrecht und gesellschaftliche Teilhabe aus rechtlicher Sicht [Age limits in labor and social law and the legal perspective of social participation]. *Zeitschrift für sozialrechtliche Praxis* 53 (7): 395.

Simitis, S. 1994. Altersdiskriminierung – die verdrängte Benachteiligung [Age discrimination – the repressed disadvantage]. *Neue Juristische Wochenzeitschrift* 22: 1453-1454.

Temming, F. 2008. *Altersdiskriminierung im Arbeitsleben: Eine rechtsmethodische Analyse [Age discrimination in working life: A legal-methodological analysis]*. München: C.H. Beck Verlag.

Tettinger, P. J. 2005. Rechtsprechungslinien des Bundesverfassungsgerichts zu Höchstaltersgrenzen als berufsbezogenen Regelungen [Jurisprudence of the Federal Constitutional Court on maximum age limits as occupational regulations]. In *Wie lange dürfen wir arbeiten?: Gesetzliche Altersgrenzen als Verfassungsproblem [What's our age limit in working life?: Legal age limits as a constitutional problem]*, eds. C. O. Lenz, T. Mann, A. Nußberger, P. J. Tettinger, O. Wulff, 85-110. Sankt Augustin: Konrad-Adenauer-Stiftung e.V.

Life Course and Social Participation: (Not Only) a Question of Fairness

Peter Dabrock

1 Life Course and the Limitations of Justice

A look at the life courses of individuals helps to uncover the grounds and limitations of the justice demanded of others. In doing so we can take a diachronic or synchronic perspective. By *diachronic perspective* I mean a person's life course over time. By *synchronic perspective* I mean the co-existence of different life courses at a certain point in time. The diachronic perspective suggests that justice is grounded in the protection and respect of individual dignity. Accordingly, it has an intrinsic relationship to freedom. The synchronic perspective in turn elucidates that freedom is not possible without the existence, availability and use of a social network created by individuals. If freedom and social participation in the life course rely on each other mutually, then justice represents a necessary but insufficient social obligation to strengthen individuals and foster social cohesion. Precisely those who want to make justice strong need to consider care and solidarity. Later I will argue that solidarity can be understood in terms of giving and gratitude.

In providing a succinct but sufficient presentation of the relationship between freedom, social participation and justice, I have decided to take two shortcuts.[1] First, I do not pursue the diachronic perspective any further here. Despite the many different understandings and interpretations of justice I hope it will be clear enough that the chance to participate in social communication is a chance to realise communicative freedom, and that this communicative freedom contains a dignity-based

[1]For a more detailed discussion of this idea and the relevant literature, see Dabrock (2012), pp. 287–338.

P. Dabrock (✉)
Friedrich-Alexander Universität Erlangen-Nürnberg, Philosophische Fakultät und Fachbereich Theologie, Erlangen, Germany
e-mail: peter.dabrock@fau.de

B. Schmitz-Luhn, C. Woopen (eds.), *Justice over the Course of Life*, Schriften zu Gesundheit und Gesellschaft - Studies on Health and Society 1,
https://doi.org/10.1007/978-3-030-86449-1_4

criterion for what a society must make available to every member independent of talents or ability over the life course.

However, this criterion demands a differentiated application: Insofar as societies have very different levels of prosperity, and insofar as individuals have different requirements over their life course as their needs change, this criterion can (or de facto must) assume very different dimensions. Accordingly, we must differentiate concepts of justice, distinguishing by age and health status, social status and cultural background, region and religion.

While I don't explore the diachronic perspective further here, my arguments are still predicated on it. This will result in the basic idea of a dignity-based criterion contained in the diachronic perspective taking form in the synchronic perspective, but also running up against limitations. This synchronic perspective emerges when one considers how life courses meet at different stages and challenge each other mutually. When generations (however constituted) meet, what should the relationship be between those social obligations traditionally called norms and values?

To this end, and in the spirit of my profession as a theologian, I will approach this very relationship by means of a short, but very influential text from the deep pre-modernity of Old Testament-era Israel: the commandment to honour thy father and mother in the Decalogue. The approach will be fashioned in an illustration-like manner, without an abstract theoretical model. This means of illustration represents my second shortcut. As with every reference to literature, such illustrations are fanned by contingency. However, this does not undercut the plausibility of this approach. Abstract theoretical models are not free of contingency either, of course. It should be immediately clear, moreover, that suggestive illustrations are not out of place with our subject matter. It is therefore of more importance how they have been translated into present-day form and how they are employed today, which also requires paying attention to their limitations.

2 The Relevance of the Old Testament's Parental Commandment

The fourth or fifth commandment of the Decalogue (depending on the counting system) is 'Honour thy father and thy mother' (Ex 20,12; Dtn 5,16). For some older people, as well as for young people brought up in the Christian church, this commandment can often elicit unpleasant memories or associations. This 'parental' commandment has been used repeatedly to legitimise familiar but socially entrenched hierarchies vis-à-vis young people or those lower in the hierarchy. Eloquent testament of this interpretation can be found in Luther's catechisms, in which the reformer traces the origins of obedience to secular authority from the parental commandment.

Having a closer look at the original intention of the commandment—and here we can be thankful for critical historical exegesis—we discover very interesting positions for the synchronic and diachronic views of how obligations and life course determine behaviour. First, the Decalogue in general and the parental commandment in particular espouse neither a world ethic (Küng 1990) nor a collection of natural laws nor a universal morality independent of age, position, sex, and ability. Rather, the Ten Commandments were directed toward male Israelites who owned and worked the land and hence were capable of holding rights. (This is why Luther likened the Ten Commandments to a Jewish version of the customary law book the *Sachsenspiegel*.) The Decalogue stipulates how life for young and old should be so as to foster the community. The Decalogue does not only prescribe rights and duties drawn from years of experience but also attaches the commandments to a notion of God as liberator. According to Exodus, the book of liberation, and Deuteronomy, the book of laws, JHWH reveals himself as a giver of freedom: 'I am Yahweh your God, who brought you out of the land of Egypt, out of the house of slavery.' (Ex 20,2; cf. Dtn 5,6). This is why Frank Crüsemann is right to identify the theme of the Decalogue as the 'preservation of freedom'. (Crüsemann 1993). As God gave life by liberating the Israelites from Egypt, the Israelites should use this freedom responsibly, preserving it within family and tribe and passing it down to the next generations.

By this basic instruction to understand and shape community life as that which preserves freedom, the parental commandment assumes central importance. Two details make this all the more apparent. First, it is the parental commandment, and not what many see as the more fundamental injunction *not to kill*, that begins the community commandments. Second, the parental commandment is, with the exception of the preceding commandment from the theological tablet to remember the Sabbath, the only one expressed in positive terms. Why is the parental commandment so central? Considering its addressees—adult Israelites—it can only be, as all exegetic investigations confirm, to ensure that the bearers of social responsibility uphold the right of the older generation to exist even after they can no longer work. Or, to put it in modern terms, the right of parents to live a dignified life as part of the social group.

The frequency with which the Old Testament drums in this message—no commandment is claimed in the Bible as often as the parental commandment—suggests its practical significance and urgency. It is evident that aging parents faced beatings (Ex 21,15), cursing (Ex 21,17), disdain (Ez 22,7), taunting (Prov 30,17), stealing (Prov 28,24), oppression (Prov 19,26), and expulsion (Prov 19,26)—such is the sad resume of the older generation's poor treatment at the hands of others. This is what the parental commandment tries to oppose. According to the Old Testament scholar Rainer Albertz, the parental commandment refers 'specifically to the appropriate care of aged parents with food, clothing, and shelter until they die, and to treating them with a respect and dignity equal to their position as parents despite the loss of their vitality. This ultimately includes a dignified burial.' (Albertz 1978).

If this interpretation is correct, then the parental commandment in its original meaning provides us not only with a diachronic perspective on the life course, according to which life in all its phases is to be led with dignity, or, to put it modern terms, with self-determination. Rather, a good life is not possible without others. Nobody who lives for himself lives well. Not even freedom is something one lives for oneself. Freedom is always communicative and related to the community and lived in society. The idea of absolute freedom—absolute in the literal sense of 'made separate'—is a distortion. The desire for freedom and the desire for inclusion in a community and a society are in need of each other, for each is precarious and endangered. The right to freedom, the wish for recognition and the participation in communities and society require social forms of obligation. In the Old Testament there is one expression for this: *Tzedakah,* or community loyalty (Koch 1984). It signifies fairness, solidarity and aspects of care. Tzedakah emanates from God but is also expected of people. The Decalogue serves to preserve Tzedakah, the community that fosters freedom. Its commandments aim at peace (shalom) while enabling the individual's communicative freedom.

3 Social Relations of Obligation

In our modern society—shaped by functional differentiation and ideological plurality—justice, solidarity and care describe different social obligations from those in ancient times (Höffe 2001). It is necessary to address the expectations attached to each form of obligation today, but by way of anticipation let me say what I see as obvious, namely, that a dignified life requires all three: justice, solidarity, and care.

Claims of *justice* aim at universal recognition. A person who calls a situation unjust demands that the situation be changed. Demands for justice thus demand action. This constitutes the strong structure and obligation that justice provides. It is increasingly common today to interpret justice as equal opportunity—the right to participate in social communication, to develop personally without intentionally harming others, to exercise communicative freedom. Thus, one must seek to realise social justice in a way that preserves human dignity within a given social framework (Nussbaum 2006). That is to say, for each society, one must identify the standard for social inclusion that justice demands on the basis of a fundamental respect for others.

Care and *love* occur at close range—face to face—and are shaped to a high degree by engagement, investment and emotional bonding at the personal level. Their success or failure often depends directly on individual identity. When freedom and love meet we are thoroughly vulnerable. It is therefore crucial to respect this vulnerability in protecting such relationships.

Solidarity fluctuates between the structure of justice and the spontaneity of care. This makes it challenging and difficult to categorise. We associate solidarity with obligations that go beyond the intimate sphere of care, but that do not extend as far as justice. The obligations of solidarity only apply to certain groups and hence are not absolute. Personal motivation in the area of solidarity is often greater than even the most urgent demands for justice. Something—a religion, a class, a local community, a cause—binds us with others who need our solidarity. This is a stronger, more intimate emotional bond than justice's abstract idea of inclusion for all people in a society, if not the global society as a whole.

Solidarity thus demands and motivates. Bonds of solidarity are precarious like relations of care, but they also create personal and collective identity and affective motivation. Precisely for this reason, receiving or giving solidarity generates a unique form of gratitude. Borrowing from Ricœur (2005) we might say that its uniqueness consists in in the fact that, on the one hand, the positions of the giver and receiver are not interchangeable, but that, on the other hand, the act of giving is also a kind of receiving and the act of receiving is also a kind of giving. (Anyone who has given something and felt the deep appreciation of the receiver knows this.) However, the act of giving—complicated as it is with non-interchangeable roles, functions, and forms of identity—is imperilled in every action and reaction. Therein lies the difference between acts of giving and acts of exchange. Acts of exchange are ruled by calculation, while a true gift aims at personal communication and is bereft of calculation. Anyone who gives out of calculation forfeits the possibility of giving. Whether we can ever truly give, or whether every form of giving is, theologically speaking, permeated with original sin, is rightfully open for debate. The philosopher Jacques Derrida offered some thoughts along these lines: 'At the limit, the gift as gift ought not appear as gift: either to the donee or to the donor. It cannot be gift as gift except by not being present as gift. Neither to the "one" nor to the "other". If the other perceives or receives it, if he or she keeps it as gift, the gift is annulled. But the one who gives it must not see it or know it either.' (Derrida 1992, p. 14). The basic heuristic idea of the difference between a gift that aims at personal communication and an exchange based on calculation can be understood beyond Derrida's important theoretical speculations. The uniqueness of solidarity is that it can be primarily understood as a gift and not as an exchange. As such, it represents a unique form of obligation between justice and care. For bonds of solidarity are not as emotional as bonds of love and care, but neither can they simply be reduced to absolute moral obligation. They emerge in relationships that are fragile, but which are mediated by mutual obligation and shared community, producing very distinct roles: the giver of solidarity and the receiver of solidarity.

4 Relations Between the Generations and Social Relations of Obligation

Let us now consider the relationship between life courses of differing lengths—the relationship between differing generations—with regard to justice, care and solidarity. Which of the three affords us the best understanding of the relationship between generations, especially from a political standpoint? I would like to claim that each form of obligation is important in itself as well as in its relationship to the others, but that the central role goes not to justice (as is frequently argued) but to solidarity.

Considering the meaning of care between generations, we can detect that we depend on others to give us love and care in general, but also on people to give love and care between generations: parents give children their existence, their upbringing, their community; children give to their parents by making them parents, by productively disrupting normal adult life and by inspiring in them child-like curiosity. Parents thank their children with parental life. Children thank their parents through the love of a child and in many cases by giving their parents the gift of grandchildren. What does this knowledge of care between the generations mean? A cautious formulation would probably be: neither state regulation nor solidarity at a remove can take the place of care. Talk of family as a nucleus of society is supposed to represent the conservative point of view, however, this is a reductive perspective. It is a general truth of humanity that without giving life and care and without receiving life and care in committed, long-term relationships we cannot lead a good life in the long run (Anselm and Dabrock 2014, pp. 103–116).

Turning to the meaning of the concepts of justice and solidarity between generations it can be seen that they are usually used imprecisely, as if they were synonymous and exchangeable. Given the aforementioned clarifications on the differences between justice and solidarity, it is not just a semantic blurring, but also a political blurring—one that robs us of important practical insights. I thus want to make the case for a clear distinction between them.

Where does the idea of justice direct our attention when we juxtapose different generations? The well-known call for justice between generations arises with the impression that the general level of social justice—which is to say, the level of social inclusion—is not sufficiently available for one age group relative to others.[2] Such situations cannot be prevented, so the concept of justice between generations is still useful. However, the problems of justice between individual classes and milieus, ethnic groups and sexes appear larger than the social fault lines between the generations. This raises the question whether the quick calls for justice between generations are being intentionally or—more dramatically—unintentionally abused for other purposes. Winfried Schmähl puts it as follows: 'One has the impression that the focus of the discussion on the distribution of economic resources between cohorts distracts one from the distribution of economic resources within cohorts.' (Schmähl 2004, p. 51).

Because the concept of justice between generations is so problematic in its application and methodology, the concept of solidarity shifts in the foreground in order to provide orientation. Solidarity does not gain this function solely from justice's insufficiency. Rather, my attempt to understand solidarity in terms of gratitude and gift[3] gives us a more constructive access to relationships between generations. Calls for solidarity are not only, as with calls for justice, indictments of the basic social conditions of individual life. They also seek to improve the chances of co-existence between generations through *active* engagement. Solidarity fills

[2]As in similar cases, this kind of observation only measures statistical magnitude, not particular instances. The 'old' exist just as little as the 'young'. Sex, disease, class and individual issues can clash with the age group distinction and exert considerably more influence on them. This does not mean that membership in a certain age group cannot in itself have a significant effect, however.

[3]For a more thorough discussion see Dabrock (2012).

relationships between generations with new life by way of giving and gratitude. It takes into account the different needs of each generation as well as the wealth of resources it offers. Indeed, we still can learn and still must learn quite a deal about the enormous civic bounty that each generation provides the others beyond personal care and state assistance. The fact that we not only have different generations but that different generations encounter each other at the same time represents a major opportunity, with constructive consequences at the micro-, meso- and macro-social levels. Moreover, we can and should direct similar attention to the gifts provided by different classes, ethnic groups and sexes. These diverse forms of life, which go far beyond age, also feed and transmit solidarity. I believe that seeing this diversity as a *benefit* will be both our biggest challenge and our greatest chance as we face upcoming demographic transformations.

The intellectual and material potential this society still holds should prevent us from trying to understand relationships between different generations primarily through instrumental calculation and the struggle for economic resources. Instead, we should promote the good of the non-interchangeable otherness of each life stage for itself and for the others, and the jubilant tension that can result from this kind of coexistence. An emphatic part of this coexistence is the last, less active phase of life. We must ensure that the elderly can live their lives without economic pressure or the need to justify the fact that they must depend on others. To this end, justice, solidarity and care must come together, and for this the Old Testament idea of community loyalty is a potential source of inspiration.

It is necessary that we make the general public aware of the *positive* potential of solidarity between generations, despite our knowing—or, better, because we know—that we tread on thinner normative ground than when we base our arguments only or primarily on justice. Proposals based on solidarity always run the risk of the charge of relying on particular ideas of the good, which are not as universally binding as the guidelines of the righteous. However, it is often overlooked that such guidelines are themselves shaped by specific social and historical ideas. Investments in solidarity have not only utilitarian grounds but also identity grounds. We see this in the Old Testament's idea of community loyalty, though we could just as well see it in the history of Christian piety for the poor and sick or in the history of worker solidarity.

As we productively shape the life course in synchronic and diachronic perspective—and not just secure the minimum conditions of social co-existence—I argue that a crucial task for constructively facing demographic change lies in pointing out the individual and social benefits of solidarity in concert with care and with justice. For this we will need practical and theoretical efforts—both of which **ceres** is prepared to undertake.

References

Albertz, R. 1978. Hintergrund und Bedeutung des Elterngebotes im Dekalog [Background and meaning of the Parental Commandment in the Decalogue]. *Zeitschrift für Alttestamentliche Wissenschaft* 90: 374.

Anselm, R., and P. Dabrock. 2014. Die Lebensform Familie als 'Leitbild' für Ehe und Partnerschaft [The family as a 'model' for marriage and partnership]. In *Leitbild am Ende? Der Streit um Ehe und Familie [An obsolete model? The dispute over marriage and family]*, eds. B. Laux and K. Hilpert, 103–116. Freiburg: Herder.

Crüsemann, F. 1993. *Bewahrung der Freiheit: Das Thema des Dekalogs in sozialgeschichtlicher Perspektive [The preservation of freedom: A socio-historical consideration of the Decalogue's subject]*. Gütersloh: Kaiser.

Dabrock, P. 2012. *Befähigungsgerechtigkeit: Ein Grundkonzept konkreter Ethik in fundamentaltheologischer Perspektive [The justice of empowerment: A basic concept of practical ethics considered from a fundamental theological perspective]*. Gütersloh: Gütersloher Verlagshaus.

Derrida, J. 1992. *Given Time*: I. Counterfeit Money (trans: Kamuf, P.). Chicago: The University of Chicago Press.

Höffe, O. 2001. *Demokratie im Zeitalter der Globalisierung [Democracy in an Age of Globalisation]*. München: C. H. Beck.

Koch, K. 1984. sdq. gemeinschaftstreu / heilvoll sein [Being loyal to the community / healing]. In *Theologisches Handwörterbuch zum Alten Testament [Theological Lexicon of the Old Testament]*, eds. E. Jenni, and C. Westermann 2: 507–530. München: Christian Kaiser Verlag/Zürich: Theologischer Verlag.

Küng, H. 1990. *Projekt Weltethos [The Global Ethic Project]*. München: Piper.

Nussbaum, M. C. 2006. *Frontiers of Justice: Disability. Nationality. Species Membership.* Cambridge, MA: Harvard University Press.

Ricœur, P. 2005. The Course of Recognition (trans: Pellauer, D.). Cambridge, MA: Harvard University Press.

Schmähl, W. 2004. Generationengerechtigkeit und Alterssicherung. Oder: Wie ein vieldeutiges Konzept einseitig instrumentalisiert wird [Intergenerational justice and old-age security. The one-way instrumentalization of an ambiguous concept]. In *Generationen und Gerechtigkeit [Generations and equity]*, eds. K. Burmeister, and B. Böhning, 45-61. Hamburg: VSA Verlag.

Fair Participation for Aging Employees at the Workplace

Mathilde Niehaus

In view of Germany's changing demographics and the higher retirement age, the number of older employees at the workplace will continue to rise in coming years. Companies must ask themselves how they can foster employee health and work fitness, as well as create tasks that are appropriate for aging workers (BMAS 2010). They must also eliminate discrimination against older workers and encourage the active participation of all employees. The operative term here is fairness: whether someone can work depends on fair attitudes and treatment; whether someone is motivated to work depends on the perception of fair attitudes and treatment.

In this talk I consider the extent to which older employees are willing, obligated and able to participate in working life. Do older people want to work longer, or are they unable to handle the workload? How do older people perform in the working world? Do more restrictive job qualifications have a stronger influence on performance than calendar age? How does work affect the aging process? I point out the resources older people possess, the challenges they face, and the resulting need for action. Using the automotive industry as an example, I show what fair participation for aging workers might look like.

1 Are Older People Obligated, Willing, and Able to Work?

New innovations in business and administration and structural changes in professional life have increased job qualifications and performance expectations. In future, these requirements will have to be met by a workforce that is both older as a whole and fewer in number. The societal importance of creating a fair workplace for aging

M. Niehaus (✉)
Humanwissenschaftliche Fakultät/DHR, Universität zu Köln, Köln, Germany
e-mail: mathilde.niehaus@uni-koeln.de

B. Schmitz-Luhn, C. Woopen (eds.), *Justice over the Course of Life*, Schriften zu Gesundheit und Gesellschaft - Studies on Health and Society 1,
https://doi.org/10.1007/978-3-030-86449-1_5

employees is shown by the following statistics. Only 42% of employees now believe that they will be able to carry out their current job until they reach the legal age of retirement without limitations (DGB—Index Gute Arbeit 2013). Older employees, in other words, often would like to leave the workforce before reaching retirement. The reasons for early retirement can be grouped into pull factors and push factors. Pull factors are first and foremost driven by rational considerations, such as financial incentives for early retirement. Push factors frequently force employees to do something they wouldn't otherwise do, such as leave work because of sickness, stressful work conditions and low job satisfaction (Radl 2007). Today, the main health-related reasons for early retirement are mental health problems, followed by musculoskeletal disorders. By comparison, 20 years ago musculoskeletal disorders were the main reasons for early retirement. This shift can be explained in part by advances in medicine and ergonomics.

Looking at the push factors more closely, we must look at the extent to which fitness is related to age. Studies show that people between the ages of 15 and 19 are more frequently unfit to work than workers over 54, but that the number of sick days they take is fewer than that taken by workers aged 55–59, with an average of 5.2 days versus 17.1 days (DAK 2014). Each year, the German economy loses 46 billion euros in reduced output due to unfitness for work. This equals some 1.8% of the gross national income (BAuA 2014). From an economic standpoint, it makes sense to think about whether older employees are obliged and able to work. I will now present some studies that consider the relationship between work, health, productivity, and age.

2 The Relationship Between Work, Health, Productivity, and Age

2.1 Work and Health

The relationship between work and health has many aspects and has been empirically studied multiple times. The most important stress factors are the intensity of physical labour, the lifting of heavy loads and monotonous tasks. Health care companies assume that a considerable share of health problems is work related (BKK 2008). The share varies between men and women and also varies with the health problem. Work-related risk factors as well as the circumstances of the person must also be factored in. Having a health problem does not automatically mean people are unable to work. 'Fit for work' and 'unfit for work' are the two endpoints of a continuum. Some people fall somewhere in between. It depends on the particular health problem in question and whether its symptoms adversely affect the execution of job tasks.

Many people who work have a chronic health problem. We know this because large companies collect data on these things. The car manufacturer Audi carries out yearly health checks for all employees and records their health status (Audi Checkup 2010). Its data show that the share of employees with chronic health problems increases with age, affecting more than half of those aged 50 and over. In many cases, these problems require workplace accommodations. The data also reveal that a considerable share of those at risk for chronic health problems are under 30, especially among manual labourers. To put it differently: social class can influence the health of younger and older employees alike. At the same time, their risk factors can be reduced or avoided through health education and other preventative measures.

2.2 *Performance and Age*

Empirical studies show that there are successive, age-specific changes in performance, but these changes are not necessarily for the worse. With increasing age certain areas of productivity improve, such as experience and judgement, while other types of productivity, such as speed and assimilation of information and processing, decline. What usually remains constant is the ability to concentrate and learn (Lehr 2003; Naegele 2004). Overall performance depends not on age but on a multitude of other factors, such as performance requirements at work, labour organisation, management culture, lifestyle, and concept of self (IAO 2002).

2.3 *Work and Performance*

Studies show that long-term concentration on specific tasks or processes leads to the restriction of the performance spectrum in older age, as one's ability to learn new tasks is curtailed through the lack of learning incentives. This means that the particular type of job can strongly influence the performance spectrum of older people (Naegele 2004; Frerichs 1998; Lehr 2003).

2.4 *Work and Age*

Though there are many studies on how work conditions influence heath, little attention has been paid to how they influence the aging process itself. Generally, experts believe that the biological aging process can be accelerated by years of heavy physical labour, night shift work, work in hot environments and prolonged exposure to dangerous substances (BMAS 2013). But it would be wrong to assume that people after a certain calendar age cannot perform certain professions. And the differences between individuals with increasing age do not permit across-the-board age cut-offs.

To sum up, these four factors—work, health, productivity, and age—are strongly interrelated. Low stress work environments that offer potential for development can help keep workers fit and keep older employees in the workforce. Employers and employees play an active role in ensuring favourable conditions at the workplace. If companies want to install a successful system for the management of aging employees, they have to consider these relationships.

3 The Management of Aging Employees

I now want to address the results of the PINA project, which Ralph Bruder and I carried out with the renowned German car manufacturers Adam Opel, Audi, Daimler, Mercedes-Benz in Mannheim, Evobus, Porsche, Ford Germany, Bosch and Volkswagen. The point of the project was to improve conditions for aging workers in the automotive industry given the fast, repetitive tasks and heavy manual labour for many industry workers. We found that the average age of plant employees is around 45, and that, as workers get older, the number whose health is adversely affected by the workplace increases, while the number of tasks suited for them decreases. Older workers who can no longer perform the same tasks must be assigned to a different area of manufacturing. Each company we considered has its own approach to doing this. As a rule, however, we found no strategic approach to aging employees. That is to say, in no case does management deal with aging in a top-down fashion.

The project revealed that the management of aging employees must be geared to the entire life course, and take into account preventive and compensatory measures. For instance, preventative measures must be offered to younger employees whose health is at risk. In general, many spheres of activity in a company must be considered when creating fair conditions for aging employees. It is not only about health promotion and health management, but also about in-house occupational rehabilitation, about training and moulding careers. There are many areas of improvement such as company culture (e.g. health management, indices used), human resource policy, professional development and training (mix-aged teams). Health insurance institutions can support the companies in these endeavours.

4 Summary

When is work fair to aging employees? As a rule, work is fair to aging employees when it is fair to people. According to the DGB Index, fair work conditions are 'conditions that employees describe as fostering development and as low-stress. This includes an income that people see as appropriate and proportionate to performance. Poor work quality results from conditions with no development potential, few resources, high stress and low income'.

Based on what I have presented here, we can also say that work is fair to aging employees when it avoids unnecessary stress, considers changes to performance requirements for aging employees, and is geared to the resources of employees (Kugler et al. 2015). Companies can support this by introducing a culture of learning that helps develop and maintain skills. Business leaders should be sensitive to age, value the personality of the individual and encourage health-conscious behaviour in their employees (Baumann et al. 2014).

Whether older employees can perform satisfying work while maintaining good physical and mental health depends on workplace conditions, individual views about the relationship between work and health and the framework provided by society. What is more, both employers and employees must work to promote fairness for aging workers.

References

Audi Checkup 2010: See information on the car manufacturer's health program at: https://www.audi-mediacenter.com/de/pressemitteilungen/erfolgsmodell-audi-checkup100000-vorsorgeuntersuchungen-fuer-mitarbeiter-9856. Accessed June 29, 2021

BAuA – Bundesanstalt für Arbeitsschutz und Arbeitsmedizin. 2014. Arbeitswelt im Wandel. Zahlen – Daten – Fakten [The Changing World of Work. Figures – Data – Facts]. http://www.baua.de/de/Publikationen/Broschueren/A90.html. Accessed December 2, 2020.

Baumann, G., M. Kugler, L. Hodek, and M. Niehaus. 2014. Führungskräfte als Manager im Demographischen Wandel stärken: Erfolgsfaktoren und Gestaltungsimpulse für eine erfolgreiche Sensibilisierung, Einbindung und Aktivierung [Supporting Executives as Managers in Demographic Change: Success Factors and Design Impulses for Successful Sensitization, Involvement and Activation]. In *Gestaltung der Arbeitswelt der Zukunft. 60. Kongress der Gesellschaft für Arbeitswissenschaft [Shaping the Working World of the Future. 60th Congress of the Society for Ergonomics] 2014, München*: 129–131. Dortmund: GfA-Press.

BKK Bundesverband. 2008. *Wettbewerbsvorteil Gesundheit. Kosten arbeitsbedingter Erkrankungen und Frühberentung in Deutschland [Health as Competitive Advantage. Costs of Work-Related Illnesses and Early Retirement in Germany]*. Essen.

BMAS – Bundesministerium für Arbeit und Soziales. 2010. Bericht der Bundesregierung: Aufbruch in die altersgerechte Arbeitswelt [Report of the Federal Ministry for Labor and Social Affairs: Departure into the Age-Appropriate World of Work]. http://www.bmas.de/DE/Service/Publikationen/a855-bericht-bundesregierung-aufbruch-altersgerechte-arbeitswelt.html. Accessed June 29, 2021.

BMAS – Bundesministerium für Arbeit und Soziales. 2013. *Erhalt der Beschäftigungsfähigkeit. Arbeitsmedizinische Empfehlung [Maintaining Employability. Occupational Health Recommendation]*. Bonn: Chudeck.

DAK – DAK Gesundheit. 2014. Analyse der Arbeitsunfähigkeitsdaten. Gesundheitsreport 2014. Die Rushhour des Lebens. Gesundheit im Spannungsfeld von Job, Karriere und Familie [Analysis of Data on the Incapacity to Work. Health Report 2014. The Rush Hour of Life. Health in the field of tension between job, career and family]. https://www.dak.de/dak/bundesthemen/gesundheitsreport-2014-2119690.html#/. Accessed February 19, 2021.

DGB – Index Gute Arbeit. 2013. *Repräsentativumfrage zum DGB-Index Gute Arbeit 2012 [Representative Survey on the DGB Good Work Index 2012]*. Hamburg: Zollenspieker Kollektiv GmbH.

Frerichs, F. 1998. *Älterwerden im Betrieb. Beschäftigungschancen und –risiken im demographischen Wandel [Getting Older in the Company. Employment Opportunities and Risks in Demographic Change].* Wiesbaden: VS Verlag für Sozialwissenschaften.

IAO – Fraunhofer Institut für Arbeitswissenschaft und Organisation, ed. 2002. *Demographischer Wandel in der Arbeitswelt [Demographic change in the world of work].* Stuttgart: Bundesministerium für Bildung und Forschung.

Kugler, M., G. Baumann, R. Bruder, L. Hodek, M. Niehaus, and A. Sinn-Behrendt. 2015. *Stärkung eines effektiven Alternsmanagements. Ergebnisse des Projekts „Gesund und qualifiziert älter werden in der Automobilindustrie – Partizipation und Inklusion von Anfang an" (PINA) [Strengthening Effective Ageing Management. Results of the Project 'Healthy and Qualified Ageing in the Automotive Industry – Participation and Inclusion right from the Start (PINA)].* Technische Universität Darmstadt, Universität zu Köln.

Lehr, U. 2003. *Psychologie des Alterns [Psychology of Ageing].* 7th ed. Wiebelsheim: Quelle & Meyer Verlag.

Naegele, G. 2004. Zwischen Arbeit und Rente. Gesellschaftliche Chancen und Risiken älterer Arbeitnehmer [Between Work and Retirement. Social Opportunities and Risks of Older Employees]. 2nd ed. Augsburg: MaroVerlag.

Radl, J. 2007. Individuelle Determinanten des Renteneintrittsalters [Individual Determinants of the Age of Retirement]. *Wirtschaft und Statistik* 5: 511–520.

Becoming Motivated and Competent to Perform Health-Enhancing Behaviors

Ralf Schwarzer

Health inequalities and the social gradients in health have been a major issue in the public health debate for many years, and there have been many attempts to improve health literacy and numeracy, knowledge about determinants of illness, stress, and well-being. A policy objective is to create the resources and opportunities that enable all people to maximize their capabilities and have control over their lives. Several excellent public health centers worldwide target such issues, among them the Institute of Health Equity at the University College of London (http://www.instituteofhealthequity.org/). The present paper goes beyond the description and explanation of health inequity by focusing on a narrow topic which is parsimonious health promotion programs for all, and their theoretical backdrop.

The chapter describes a theoretical approach, from which changes in health behavior can be explained and predicted, as has been shown by a variety of empirical studies. In addition, this approach provides some guidelines for the design of health promotion programs. Psychological constructs and mechanisms are presented that may be used as a backdrop for health behavior intervention designs.

In health promotion, both the behavioral and the situational prevention can be implemented. The latter is when the environment provide incentives and opportunities that were created to incite practicing healthy behaviors, for example, to refrain from alcohol and tobacco, or build healthy habits such as vegetable consumption, exercise, hygiene, and safety compliance. The public health task is to create the conditions for people to have control of their lives. This includes developing asset-based approaches which could reduce health-compromising behaviors, for example, encourage exercise outside and active travel to work and school or give credits to

R. Schwarzer (✉)
Department of Psychology, Freie Universität Berlin, Berlin, Germany

SWPS University of Social Sciences and Humanities, Warszawa, Poland
e-mail: ralf.schwarzer@fu-berlin.de

B. Schmitz-Luhn, C. Woopen (eds.), *Justice over the Course of Life*, Schriften zu Gesundheit und Gesellschaft - Studies on Health and Society 1,
https://doi.org/10.1007/978-3-030-86449-1_6

children if they eat well at school and at home. Community based approaches need to be developed alongside other effective approaches. The following section do not explicitly deal with public health policy but with interventions to change behaviors at the individual level.

1 Psychological Constructs and Mechanisms in Health Behavior Change

Refraining from health-compromising behaviors and adopting health-enhancing behaviors constitutes a psychological process that has a number of building blocks (Fig. 1). People may simply follow others (social norm), they may perceive a health risk, they may expect positive outcomes of behavior change, and they may have strong optimistic self-beliefs in being capable to initiate actions (self-efficacy). This way they become motivated (intention). But to translate their motivation into action requires planning, and to maintain the action requires action control. To assist people in moving through this change process, one can provide motivational support in the beginning and behavioral support later on.

Health psychology asks, among others, why and how people change their health behaviors. It identifies barriers and difficulties, and suggests how to influence this process. Psychology has developed scientific constructs and models to deal with these issues. A social-cognitive process model of health behavior, the Health Action Process Approach (HAPA) (Schwarzer 2008) is one such model. The HAPA assumes that the process of behavior change contains at least two phases: a motivational and volitional one. In the first one, motivational support is needed, and in the second one, behavioral support is needed.

In the motivational phase, intention formation is at stake, which means that a person becomes motivated to refrain from a health-compromising behavior or adopts a health-enhancing behavior. Subsequently, this intention must be translated into

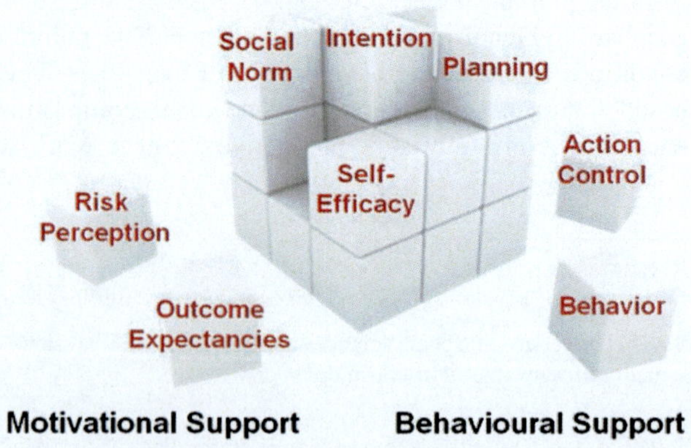

Fig. 1 Some psychological building blocks for health promotion programs

action. The post-intentional mechanisms of planning, adopting, and maintaining the target behavior will take place in the volitional phase. In both phases, different social-cognitive variables and mechanisms are dominant. The intention formation in the motivational phase are mainly influenced by action-outcome expectancies, and perceived self-efficacy and, more distal and to a lesser degree, also by some risk perception. In the initiation and maintenance of the behavior (in the volitional phase), planning, action control, and also self-efficacy are important predictors. This will be explained in more detail below.

1.1 Motivational Phase: Risk Perception, Outcome Expectancies, Motivational Self-Efficacy

People in the pre-intentional phase usually do not give much thought about their behavior and may not be aware of the potential risks when continuing their health-compromising behaviors. Due to a lack of intention to change their behavior, they shall be called "unmotivated". The level of motivation can be influenced by changing the risk perception (e.g. after medical feedback about an existing risk such as high blood pressure), the action-outcome expectancy (e.g. positive consequences after changing), and self-efficacy (e.g. confidence in one's capability to change). However, risk perception alone is not sufficient to form an intention, but merely a possible beginning of the motivation process. The action-outcome expectancy refers to the anticipated consequences of a possible change in behavior, with positive and negative consequences leading to a decisional balance. Dominant positive expectations regarding a health behavior favors the formation of the intention, but only if a certain level of self-efficacy is given. Self-efficacy is the subjective conviction to perform certain challenging behaviors and to reach one's goal due to one's own competence, even if barriers emerge.

When it comes, for example among unmotivated people, to promote the daily consumption of at least five servings of fruits or vegetables, then one can begin to address the implications of an unhealthy diet by providing risk feedback. However, this has virtually no effect, if it is not accompanied by the other two factors. One has to communicate the favorable consequences of consumption, e.g., on body self-concept, physical fitness, or appearance (action-outcome expectations). In addition, the ability of changing one's diet needs to be emphasized. Self-efficacy can be improved by reinforcing the first steps to mastery experience, by providing role models (testimonials of others who have been successful), and also by persuading people that they really can do it.

1.2 Volitional Phase: Planning, Self-Efficacy, Action Control

People who have already made a decision to change a certain behavior, but still show no behavioral initiation shall be called "intenders". They often have difficulties in translating their intentions into concrete behavior. Planning has been found to mediate between intention and behavior. There are two main ways of mental simulation: action planning and coping planning. Their inclusion in intervention designs has proven to be effective in many studies (for an overview see Hagger and Luszczynska 2014). An action plan refers to the when, where and how of a particular behavior, e.g., "I plan to run on Sunday morning at 10 a.m. with my friend for half an hour through the park". After persons have planned when, where and how the action is supposed to take place, they can anticipate potential obstacles and develop strategies to overcome these which is called coping planning. When planning an action in the volitional phase, also self-efficacy beliefs play an important role. The number and quality of the generated action plans depend on one's own perceived competence and experience to perform planned actions. As soon as the target behavior is initiated, the actional phase takes place, in which the adoption and maintenance of the behavior are at stake. Such a process is not possible through a single act of will, but includes a variety of self-regulatory skills and strategies. Such volitional factors are strategic planning and recovery self-efficacy that need to be taken into account.

In contrast to the prospective planning, action control is a retrospective or concurrent self-regulatory mechanism by recording one's behavior and comparing it with the previously set objectives is (with self-monitoring as its main component). The volitional process also includes the preparation for the action, for example, shopping healthy foods, purchasing sports equipment, or making appointments for the execution of the target activity.

When it comes, for example, to promote the daily consumption of at least five servings of fruits or vegetables at already motivated people, then one can begin to develop plans, writing explicitly about the when, where and how ("On Tuesday morning at 10 clock I eat an apple in the office"). After action planning, barriers should be identified ("What do I do if I am then just called to the boss?"), resulting in coping plans to meet the requirements (". . . .then I take an extra portion of salad at lunch in the canteen"). Maintaining the behavior is supported by use of a daily diary in the form of a simple calendar, recording all consumed portions of fruit or vegetables every evening (action control). And of course, self-efficacy needs to be further cultivated by feedback on mastery experience.

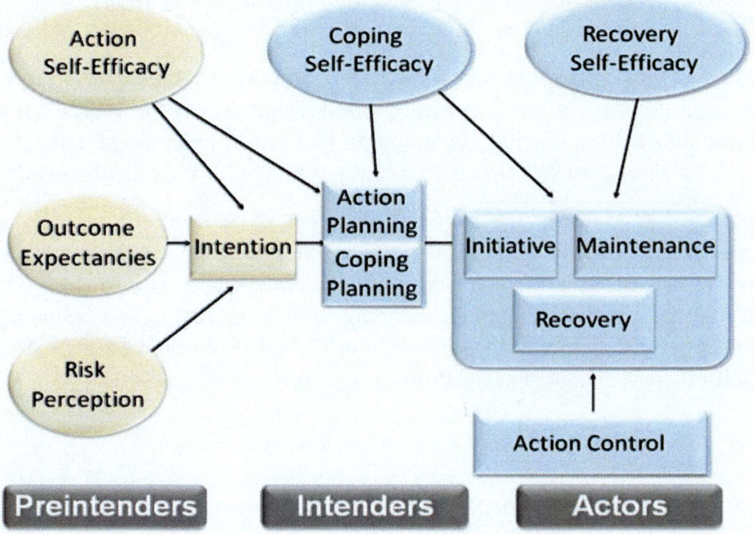

Fig. 2 Diagram of the Health Action Process Approach (HAPA) (Schwarzer 2008). Arrows represent causal paths, text at bottom of figure represents different phases of action

1.3 The Structure of the Health Action Process Approach (HAPA) at a Glance

The model (see Fig. 2) combines continuum and stage-theoretical assumptions. As a continuum model (mediator model) it is suitable for the analysis and prediction of behavior change. Path analyses are usually specified that determine the empirical weights of the model-involved parameters.

HAPA can be briefly characterized by the following main principles.

Principle 1: Motivation and Volition The health behavior change process is divided into two phases. There is a switch of mindsets when people move from deliberation to action. First comes the motivation phase in which people develop their intentions. Afterwards, they enter the volition phase.

Principle 2: Two Volitional Phases In the volition phase, there are two groups of people: those who have not yet translated their intentions into action, and those who have. Thus, there are inactive as well as active persons in this phase. In other words, in the volitional phase one finds intenders as well as actors who are characterized by different psychological states. Thus, in addition to viewing health behavior change as a continuous process, one can also create three categories of people with different mindsets, depending on their current location within the course of behavior change: preintenders, intenders, and actors. This segmentation serves to develop matching treatments.

Principle 3: Postintentional Planning Intenders who are in the volitional preactional stage are motivated to change, but they do not act because they might lack the correct skills to translate their intention into action. Planning is a key strategy at this point. It serves as an operative mediator between intentions and behavior.

Principle 4: Two Kinds of Mental Simulation Planning can be divided into action planning and coping planning. Action planning pertains to the when, where, and how of intended action. Coping planning includes the anticipation of barriers and the design of alternative actions that help to attain one's goal in spite of impediments.

Principle 5: Phase-Specific Self-Efficacy Perceived self-efficacy is required throughout the entire process. However, the nature of self-efficacy differs from phase to phase. This is because there are different challenges as people progress from one phase to the next one. Goal setting, planning, initiation, action, and maintenance all pose challenges that are not of the same nature. Therefore, one can distinguish between action self-efficacy, maintenance self-efficacy, and recovery self-efficacy.

2 Interventions Based on the Health Action Process Approach (HAPA)

For the development of interventions, one often segments the audience into three groups in terms of their stages of change: unmotivated, motivated, and already acting individuals. This subdivision makes it possible to tailor interventions to the variables that are relevant in each stage. Statistically, the stage acts as moderator: within each stage a different intervention component is considered to dominantly affect the mindsets of participants. For example, unmotivated persons seem to benefit from positive action-outcome-expectancies, motivated ones benefit from planning, and actors benefit from action control. Stage models allow for an optimal fit between personal characteristics and types of intervention. Table 1 provides an overview of the main constructs that play a role at the three major stages of behavior change where people are labelled as preintenders, intenders, and actors.

Large-scale HAPA projects were conducted mainly on diet and exercise in the context of cardiovascular or diabetes risk reduction programs such as

- the Melbourne Diabetes Prevention Study (MDPS) (Davis-Lameloise et al. 2013),
- the German Railway metabolic syndrome prevention study (Fleig et al. 2010),
- the Greater Green Triangle Diabetes Prevention Project (Laatikainen et al. 2007),
- the GOAL implementation study (Absetz et al. 2007),
- the Norfolk Diabetes Prevention Study (Murray et al. 2011),
- the Waste the Waist study (Gillison et al. 2012),
- the FABA cardiac and orthopedic rehabilitation study (Fleig et al. 2011; Fleig et al. 2013),
- the Berlin cardiac rehabilitation study (Sniehotta et al. 2006),
- the Berlin Stays Fit study (older women fitness program) (Evers et al. 2012), and
- the Iranian Physical Activity Maintenance in Rehabilitation Project (Aliabad et al. 2014).

Table 1 Intervention matrix for health action process approach (HAPA)-based stage-specific treatments

	Stage of Change Group		
	Preintender	Intender	Actor
Motivational Constructs			
Self-efficacy (motivational)	X		
Risk perception	X		
Outcome expectancies	X		
Goal setting	X		
Volitional Constructs			
Action planning		X	X
Coping planning		X	X
Self-efficacy (maintenance)		X	X
Self-efficacy (recovery)			X
Action control			X

Fig. 3 Areas where HAPA-based global 10-minute health behavior interventions have been implemented successfully

3 Examples of 10-Minute Global Health Behavior Interventions

If individual-level interventions are designed with the purpose in mind to reach a large audience, they must be brief, precise, context-specific, and theory-based. Sometimes, very brief ones can be effective, for example a one-minute intervention to change oral self-care (Sniehotta et al. 2006). We have designed such interventions that take about 10–20 min and implemented them in seven countries (see Fig. 3).

Behavioral domains have been physical activity, fruit and vegetable consumption, dental flossing, hand hygiene, and sun screen use. Figure 4 displays one page of a three-page leaflet as an example page of a volitional intervention to promote fruit and vegetable consumption in India (Lhakhang et al. 2014). Participants generate action plans in the upper part, and coping plans in the lower part, and on the right-hand side, plan-specific self-efficacy is assessed.

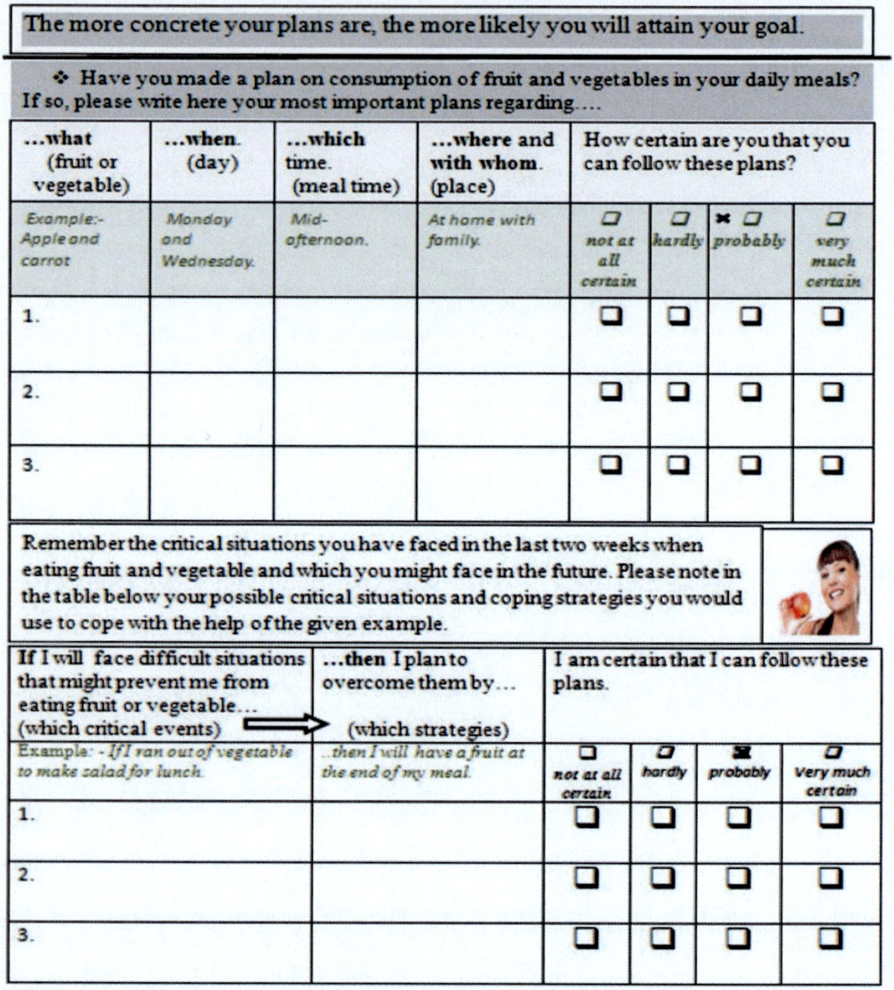

The more concrete your plans are, the more likely you will attain your goal.

❖ Have you made a plan on consumption of fruit and vegetables in your daily meals? If so, please write here your most important plans regarding....

...what (fruit or vegetable)	...when. (day)	...which time. (meal time)	...where and with whom. (place)	How certain are you that you can follow these plans?			
Example:- Apple and carrot	*Monday and Wednesday.*	*Mid-afternoon.*	*At home with family.*	❑ *not at all certain*	❑ *hardly*	✖ ❑ *probably*	❑ *very much certain*
1.				❑	❑	❑	❑
2.				❑	❑	❑	❑
3.				❑	❑	❑	❑

Remember the critical situations you have faced in the last two weeks when eating fruit and vegetable and which you might face in the future. Please note in the table below your possible critical situations and coping strategies you would use to cope with the help of the given example.

If I will face difficult situations that might prevent me from eating fruit or vegetable... (which critical events) ⇨	...then I plan to overcome them by... (which strategies)	I am certain that I can follow these plans.			
Example: - *If I ran out of vegetable to make salad for lunch*	*..then I will have a fruit at the end of my meal*	❑ *not at all certain*	❑ *hardly*	✖ *probably*	❑ *Very much certain*
1.		❑	❑	❑	❑
2.		❑	❑	❑	❑
3.		❑	❑	❑	❑

Fig. 4 Example page of a leaflet-based volitional intervention to promote fruit and vegetable consumption in India (Lhakhang et al. 2014). Participants generate action plans in the upper part, and coping plans in the lower part, and on the right-hand side, plan-specific self-efficacy is assessed

4 Taking Advantage of Information and Communication Technology (ICT) Such as Social Media

Another approach to yield a maximum reach of interventions lies in the information and communication technology (ICT). Public health promotion can benefit from ICT based interventions such as text messaging and online courses (eHealth) as well as smartphone apps (mHealth) (Joseph et al. 2014). Technologies may offer strong

Fig. 5 Example page of a German online smoking cessation program that is free of charge and has attracted a large audience (Schwarzer and Satow 2012)

support for health behavior change. The availability of thousands of downloadable mHealth apps facilitates the adoption of devices to self-monitor health behaviors and conditions. This will allow users to track their goal setting and goal striving, changes in social-cognitive variables, plans, and actual health behaviors. Information becomes easily accessible and interpretable. Web-linked devices offer a continuous environment for the access of text, image, audio and other types of structured and semi-structured information. Built-in social media elements offer a wealth of social support options. Tracking performance coupled with powerful decision support techniques, provides a dependable, information-rich profile of individuals as they pass through the behavior change process. Figure 5 shows an example page of a German online smoking cessation program that is free of charge and has attracted a large audience (Schwarzer and Satow 2012).

Combining HAPA with ICT may optimize stratified behavior interventions to enhance self-engagement and self-monitoring (Lyons et al. 2014; Soureti et al. 2011) because more frequent diagnostics allow to tailor for individual needs. Users need

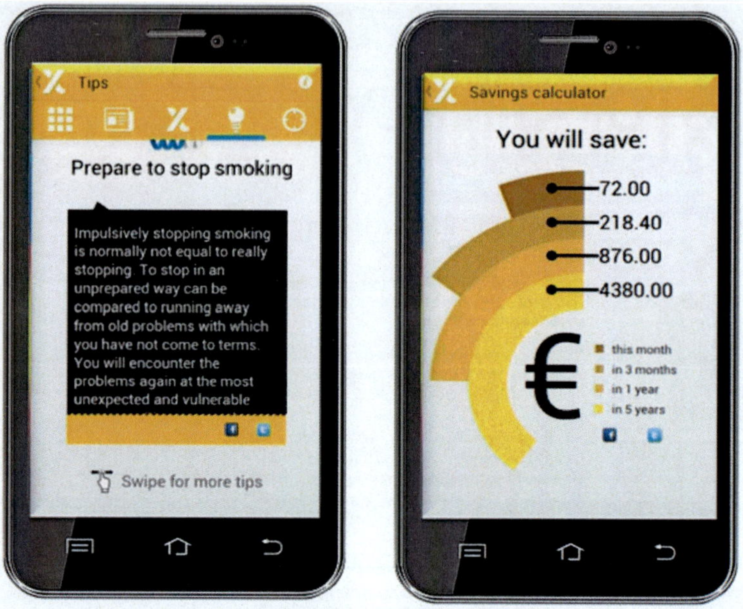

Fig. 6 Example of mHealth application to reduce smoking, the "Exsmokers iCoach" (http://www.exsmokers.eu/)

behavioral support to overcome obstacles and maintain health behaviors after initiation. Here, a number of behavior change techniques can be applied to support planning, action control, and maintenance self-efficacy. The advanced technology allows for immediate feedback loops that keep users online, monitoring lapses as well as progress and providing resource information that is individually tailored. There are lots of mHealth applications available, among them many that address smoking cessation (Choi et al. 2014). Figure 6 shows an example of a mHealth application to reduce smoking, the "Exsmokers iCoach" (http://www.exsmokers.eu/).

5 Conclusions

Overall, the HAPA is to be regarded neither as a rigid stage model nor as a classic mediator model, but rather as a flexible hybrid framework that provides the starting points for further research and evidence-based, theory-driven orientation to promote health behavior. The application of psychological constructs to processes of behavior change leads to a better understanding of these processes and provides guidance for the design of health promotion. Interventions should be the more effective, the more they are tailored to homogeneous groups of addressees.

References

Absetz, P., R. Valve, B. Oldenburg, H. Heinonen, A. Nissinen, M. Fogelholm, V. Ilvesmäki, M. Talja, and A. Uutela. 2007. Type 2 Diabetes Prevention in the "Real World": One-Year Results of the GOAL Implementation Trial. *Diabetes Care* 30: 2465–2470.

Aliabad, H. O., M. Vafaeinasab, M. A. Morowatisharifabad, S. A. Afshani, M. G. Firoozabadi, and S. K. Forouzannia. 2014. Maintenance of Physical Activity and Exercise Capacity After Rehabilitation in Coronary Heart Disease: A Randomized Controlled Trial. *Global Journal of Health Science* 6 (6): 198–208. https://doi.org/10.5539/gjhs.v6n6p198.

Choi J., G. Y. Noh, and D. J. Park. 2014. Smoking Cessation Apps for Smartphones: Content Analysis With the Self-Determination Theory. *Journal of Medical Internet Research* 16 (2): e44. https://doi.org/10.2196/jmir.3061.

Davis-Lameloise, N., A. Hernan, E. D. Janus, E. Stewart, R. Carter, C. M. Bennett, S. O'Reilly, B. Philpot, E. Vartiainen, and J. A. Dunbar. 2013. Dunbar and Melbourne Diabetes Prevention Study (MDPS) research group. The Melbourne Diabetes Prevention Study (MDPS): study protocol for a randomized controlled trial. *Trials* 14, Article 31. https://doi.org/10.1186/1745-6215-14-31.

Evers, A., V. Klusmann, R. Schwarzer, and I. Heuser. 2012. Adherence to physical and mental activity interventions: coping plans as a mediator and prior adherence as a moderator. *British Journal of Health Psychology* 17 (3): 477–491. https://doi.org/10.1111/j.2044-8287.2011.02049.x.

Fleig, L., S. Lippke, S. Pomp, and R. Schwarzer. 2011. Exercise maintenance after rehabilitation: How experience can make a difference. *Psychology of Sport and Exercise* 12 (3): 293–299. https://doi.org/10.1016/j.psychsport.2011.01.003.

Fleig, L., S. Lippke, A. U. Wiedemann, J. P. Ziegelmann, T. Reuter, and C. Gravert. 2010. Förderung von körperlicher Aktivität im betrieblichen Kontext: Ein randomisiertes Kontrollgruppen-Design zur Untersuchung von stadienspezifischen Interventionseffekten [Promoting physical activity in a workplace setting: A randomized control trial investigating stage-specific intervention effects]. *Zeitschrift für Gesundheitspsychologie* 18 (2): 69–78.

Fleig, L., S. Pomp, L. Parschau, M. Barz, D. Lange, R. Schwarzer, and S. Lippke. 2013. From intentions via planning and behavior to physical exercise habits. *Psychology of Sport and Exercise* 14 (5): 632–639.

Gillison F., C. J. Greaves, A. Stathi, R. Ramsay, P. Bennett, G. Taylor, M. Francis, and R. Chandler. 2012. "Waste the waist": the development of an intervention to promote changes in diet and physical activity for people with high cardiovascular risk. *British Journal of Health Psychology* 17 (2): 327–345.

Hagger, M. S., and A. Luszczynska. 2014. Implementation intention and action planning interventions in health contexts: State of the research and proposals for the way forward. *Applied Psychology: Health and Well-Being* 6: 1–47.

Joseph, R. P., N. H. Durant, T. J. Benitez, and D. W. Pekmezi. 2014. Internet-Based Physical Activity Interventions. *American Journal of Lifestyle Medicine* 8 (1): 42–68. https://doi.org/10.1177/1559827613498059.

Laatikainen, T., J. A. Dunbar, A. Chapman, A. Kilkkinen, E. Vartiainen, S. Heistaro, B. Philpot, P. Absetz, S. Bunker, A. O'Neil, P. Reddy, J. D. Best, and E. D. Janus. 2007. Prevention of Type 2 Diabetes by lifestyle intervention in an Australian primary health care setting: Greater Green Triangle (GGT) Diabetes Prevention Project. *BMC Public Health* 7: 249–256. https://doi.org/10.1186/1471-2458-7-249.

Lhakhang, P., M. Gholami, N. Knoll, and R. Schwarzer. 2014. Comparing an Educational with a Self-Regulatory Intervention to Adopt a Dental Flossing Regimen. *Psychology, Health and Medicine* 20 (4): 381–392. https://doi.org/10.1080/13548506.2014.951368.

Lyons, E. J., Z. H. Lewis, B. G. Mayrsohn, and J. L. Rowland. 2014. Behavior Change Techniques Implemented in Electronic Lifestyle Activity Monitors: A Systematic Content Analysis. *Journal of Medical Internet Research* 16 (8): e192. https://doi.org/10.2196/jmir.3469.

Murray, N., S. Abadi, A. Blair, M. Dunk, and M. J. Sampson. 2011. The importance of type 2 diabetes prevention: The Norfolk Diabetes Prevention Study. *British Journal of Diabetes and Vascular Disease* 11: 308–313.

Schwarzer, R. 2008. Modeling health behavior change: How to predict and modify the adoption and maintenance of health behaviors. *Applied Psychology: An International Review* 57 (1): 1–29. https://doi.org/10.1111/j.1464-0597.2007.00325.x.

Schwarzer, R., and L. Satow. 2012. Online intervention engagement predicts smoking cessation. *Preventive Medicine* 56: 233–236. https://doi.org/10.1016/j.ypmed.2012.07.006.

Sniehotta, F. F., U. Scholz, and R. Schwarzer. 2006. Action plans and coping plans for physical exercise: A longitudinal intervention study in cardiac rehabilitation. *British Journal of Health Psychology* 11: 23–37.

Soureti, A., P. Murray, M. Cobain, M. Chinapaw, W. van Mechelen, and R. Hurling. 2011. Exploratory Study of Web-Based Planning and Mobile Text Reminders in an Overweight Population. *Journal of Medical Internet Research* 13 (4): e118.

Autonomy and Care in the Law of the Human Biography

Reinhard Damm

1 Personal Law and Human Lives

This lecture deals with the subject of autonomy and care in the law governing human life, which, from a juridical perspective, is chiefly but not only part of an area of law known in German legal terminology as "law of persons". It includes rules on personal status and legal capacity (including the capacity of having rights and duties) as well as rules governing the "capacity to act" as a capacity to effectively perform legal actions—that is, the capacity to generate rights and duties through one's own actions.[1] Concerning the first aspect of personal status, a few observations should be made. Afterwards we will address the subject of legal capacity to act in the context of self-determination and care.

Regarding personal status and legal capacity, we should begin by asking: who or what is actually under consideration here as a *subject of human life*? This entails the

Completion of the manuscript on 4 June 2015. Cf. since then: Damm, Information und Wissen im Recht der modernen Medizin - Aufstieg und Krise des informed consent, in: Katzenmeier (ed.), *Medizin* - Recht - Wissenschaft. Festschrift für Dieter Hart, 2020, p. 81 ff; Damm, Empirie der Einwilligungsfähigkeit. Zum Verhältnis von professionsinterner Regelbildund und Recht aus deutscher Sicht, in: Bernat/Grabenwarter/Kneihs/Pöschl/Stöger/Wiederin/Zahrl (eds.), Festschrift für Christian Kopetzki, 2019, p. 105 ff; Damm, Assistierte Selbstbestimmung als normatives und empirisches Problem des Rechts - am Beispiel von Einwilligungs- und Entscheidungsfähigkeit, Zeitschrift für Rechtssoziologie 2017, p. 337 ff; Damm, Einwilligungs- und Entscheidungsfähigkeit in der Entwicklung von Medizin und Medizinrecht, MedR 2015, p. 775 ff.

[1] Wolf/Neuner, *Allgemeiner Teil des Bürgerlichen Rechts*, 10th ed., 2012, pp. 116 ff., pp. 126 ff.

R. Damm (✉)
Universität Bremen, Fachbereich Rechtswissenschaft, Bremen, Germany
e-mail: rdamm@uni-bremen.de

B. Schmitz-Luhn, C. Woopen (eds.), *Justice over the Course of Life*, Schriften zu Gesundheit und Gesellschaft - Studies on Health and Society 1,
https://doi.org/10.1007/978-3-030-86449-1_7

further question as to whether we should be discussing *subjects, persons,* or *human beings.* This alone would be a complicated subject. Not coincidentally, both the German Civil Code (§§ 1 ff *Bürgerliches Gesetzbuch* [BGB]) as well as the constitution (Articles 1 & 2 *Grundgesetz* [GG]) place "human being," "person" and "personality" prominently at the beginning of each text. To a certain extent, this involves the *legal constitution of the person* and the *constitutional law of persons* as a basis for the legal system as such. This also includes their importance in relation to personal life histories. If a comprehensive "cradle to grave" scope is assumed of the civil code according to the traditional interpretation, especially with reference to life histories—that is, starting with § 1 (the beginning of legal capacity upon birth) and continuing on to the last volume (inheritance law)—then this representation has become largely obsolete owing to advances in medicine, if nothing else. Therefore, we should consider not only "long life" in the sense relevant to the conference topic here, but rather empirical and normative extensions of the life-span in *both* directions—"forward" and "backward," as it were. And not only that: there are now already debates concerning controversies such as *prenatal legal subjectivity* and *postmortal legal subjectivity*—or postmortal *protection of personality rights*, at any rate.[2] All of this, in fact, would be perfectly topical, but not in the extensive format of this presentation.

In what follows, we will examine two subject areas: first, persons and populations at the endpoints of the human life-cycle will be the focus (II). Thus, we are here discussing *the young and the old* and hence, categories of persons, in whose case the relationship between self-determination and care can become a particular source of tension, rendering "health competence" especially problematic. In the section after that (III), we will examine some issue-specific aspects relating to medical specialties. And finally, some thoughts on the problems of and perspectives on the formulation of norms will be outlined (IV). Given the research interest of the author, it is obvious that the topic will be handled from the vantage point of *civil law* and *medical law.* The subject-matter deals especially with the capacity to act in the sense of capacity to consent in matters involving the effective performance of legal acts—in this case, in the medical/health field—and along with that, the law of persons in the further sense described.

[2]Wolf/Neuner, *ibid.*, pp. 118 f., pp. 123 f., at the end of legal capacity and postmortal protection of personality rights.

2 Persons and Populations at the Endpoints of the Human Biography

2.1 *Autonomy Problems with the Young and the Old*

Autonomy is one of the "big stories" of recent times and "self-determination" is even regarded as the "decisive, constitutive principle of the modern era".[3] It is also regarded as a big story in recent legal history and probably as one of the biggest stories in the recent history of medical law. Self-determination, in the context of the development and use of new medical options, is now ubiquitous in the generating of normative rules. This story has been recited so forcefully that by now the inevitable doubts are starting to surface regarding its unproportionate relevance or even repressive dominance over other normative rationales. There has been talk of an inappropriate "fixation on autonomy in medical and bioethics" and of a "downgrading—if not an upending—of social responsibility".[4] In this context, the issue of "care" as a competing and corrective theme is also brought to the fore, not least as an additional guiding principle of medical intervention for the benefit of patients. So "self-determination and care" are now frequently conceptually linked together, thus becoming a dual-tracked guide to action, balancing the *autonomy* of patients with their *well-being*.

Moreover, we are addressing—let it be emphasized again—*both* endpoints of life when referring to *the* end or inflection points of the human life-cycle, thus taking into account not only the *elderly* (when in need of care or suffering from dementia, for example), but the *young* as well, including both children and adolescents. And so we are slightly diverging in emphasis from the rather age-specific tone and tenor of this particular conference. The reasoning is twofold: First, we are pointing out once again the issue of extending life-spans in *both* directions ("forwards" and "backwards") to some extent. This includes the trend in favor of enhancing and upgrading *health competence* for young people who have yet to reach maturity. Here we are addressing the extension of the *capacity and burden of decision-making* of the young, which also involves health competence. Life is therefore not to be regarded as a "long life" just because and when an advanced age is reached; rather, there are also extensions of one's own life lived "forwards", insofar as it is a matter of early or earlier choices between autonomy and demands made from without. In light of this, the second line of reasoning aims at *structural parallels of the formulation of norms* and the beginning and end phases of human lives. And in this regard—this point is of great significance—special problems arise when dealing with *self-determination and care*—this point is of great significance. Not coincidentally and with justice did the German Ethics Council (*Deutscher Ethikrat*) in its statement on "Dementia and Self-

[3]Hollerbach, *Selbstbestimmung und Recht*, Sitzungsberichte der Heidelberger Akademie der Wissenschaften. Philosophisch-historische Klasse, 1996, p. 25.

[4]Both of these citations were taken from the invitation to the annual convention of the *Akademie für Ethik in der Medizin*, 2010.

determination"[5] perhaps somewhat surprisingly emphasize that the "increasing self-determination in the case of children" was also of relevance in the formulation of norms to the field of senile dementia. In a more comprehensive sense, this is about the relationship between self-determination and care, which has been increasingly discussed by medicine, medical ethics and medical law in recent times, in the case of especially vulnerable persons in need of protection, who allegedly or in fact have problems involving limited (cognitive/mental) capabilities and as a result, deficient volitional and decision-making competence—either supposedly or actually.

2.2 *Minor Patients: Children and Adolescents*

2.2.1 Competency and Limitations, Especially on the Concept of Capacity for Consent

Children and adolescents are to be found in virtually every list of problems related to the balancing act between self-determination and care. In this sense, we are not only concerned with "long life", as in the motto of the conference, but also with "short life". When considering this category of persons, it is therefore—from the standpoint of classic civil law, the new medical law as well as our inquiry into "medical competence"—very much a matter of qualifications and limitations, i.e. *legal capacity, contractual competence as well as the capacity for consent,* and numerous other relevant issues. There is a consensus, however, that this group of people poses some special legal problems at both the empirical as well as the normative levels. The law as it relates to minors is traditionally a matter of protecting their rights. That notwithstanding, this designation especially applies to the area of *asset and market-related legal competence*.[6]

In the realm of strictly personal decisions—particularly in the case of medical procedures—things are different. Of paramount importance for medical law, and especially the category of persons under consideration at present, is therefore the normative concept of *legal capacity to reason and give consent.*[7] This is not simply a minor problem of detail, but rather a very representative element of the law of persons as it specifically relates to medicine. In certain situations, it determines the

[5] German Ethics Council, *Demenz und Selbstbestimmung*, 2012, p. 64.

[6] Incidentally, we should remember that the lowering of the age of majority from 21 to 18 (§ 2 BGB) in 1974 already marked a notable expansion of self-determination for a category of persons previously rather limited in their contractual capacity.

[7] An overview of the subject can found in Wolf/Neuner, *id.*, pp. 128 ff; Ellenberger in: Palandt, *Bürgerliches Gesetzbuch*, 73rd ed., 2014, summary of § 104, margin num. 8; Weidenkaff in: Palandt, *id.*, § 630d, margin num. 3; originally in Ohly, "*Volenti non fit iniuria*". *Die Einwilligung im Privatrecht*, 2002; specifically in a medical context most recently again in Gleixner-Eberle, *Die Einwilligung in die medizinische Behandlung Minderjähriger. Eine arztrechtliche Untersuchung im Rechtsvergleich mit Österreich und der Schweiz sowie mit Blick auf das Internationale Privat- und Strafrecht*, 2014.

boundary between autonomy and heteronomy, particularly in connection with medical procedures.[8] This is a *cross-generational criterion* for determining health competence which can be applied regardless of age. Despite repeated indications of a need for a more precise specification of this concept as it was formulated, legislators up till now have "shirked" their duty.[9] This is "surprisingly"[10] also true of the *Patients' Rights Law* of 2013, the sections amending §§ 630a ff BGB of which contain neither a conceptual clarification of the capacity for consent, nor, for example, any rules on the problematic and controversial case of the existing capacity for consent possessed by minors and the elderly.[11] For this reason, the preponderance of the case law does also require the consent of a custodial guardian when an underage patient has decision-making capacity.[12] In the secondary literature, some objections have been raised against this. It has been pointed out that, according to prevailing opinion, adults capable of giving consent can always make these decisions for themselves, without necessarily involving a guardian or a health care proxy.[13] Here some see a "suspect case of discrimination":[14]

> However desirable consensus on decisions between parents and underage children may actually be, it should nevertheless be born in mind that giving legal representatives—even parents—a veto over persons with the capacity to make decisions, give consent and exercise self-determination restricts their constitutionally guaranteed rights. Therefore, there should only be a requirement for (necessary) mutual decisions in the case of persons capable of communicating, but not of giving consent—be they minors or of legal age. In cases of conflict, persons capable of giving consent should be able to make the decisions for themselves, even if they are underage.[15]

As the legislature has refused to give any substantive definition to the concept of capacity for consent, we are left with the formulaic definitions of the judiciary. The precedent was set by the Federal Court of Justice in 1958, which dealt with the question of whether a minor "is capable of gauging the meaning and importance of the medical procedure and his consent thereunto in accordance with his/her mental and moral maturity".[16] The main *political thrust*, however, aims at avoiding the

[8] Cf. from the standpoint of "geriatric law" Spickhoff's important article: *Autonomie und Heteronomie im Alter, Archiv für die civilistische Praxis* 208, 2008, pp. 345 ff.

[9] Coester-Waltjen, *Reichweite und Grenzen der Patientenautonomie von Jungen und Alten – ein Vergleich, Medizinrecht* 2012, p. 553.

[10] Gleixner-Eberle, *id.*, p. 453. Nevertheless, patients without the capacity for consent are referred to in the context of consent in § 630d I, 2.

[11] Recently addressed by Gleixner-Eberle, *id.*, pp. 453 ff.; Katzenmeier, *Patientenrechte und Arzthaftung, Karlsruher Forum 2013,* 2014, p. 24.

[12] German Supreme Court (BGH), *Neue Juristische Wochenschrift*, 2007, p. 217.

[13] Spickhoff, *Archiv für die civilistische Praxis* 208, 2008, p. 389.

[14] Cf. Spickhoff, *Archiv für die civilistische Praxis* 208, 2008, p. 389; on the "equal-treatment argument" when comparing both minors capable to understand and adults, see also: Coester-Waltjen, *Medizinrecht* 2012, pp. 557 f.

[15] Spickhoff, *Archiv für die civilistische Praxis* 208, 2008, pp. 389 f.

[16] *Bundesgerichtshof /Zivilsachen* 29, p. 33.

schematically rigid age limits of contract law in situations of a strictly personal nature. This, though, comes at the cost of an *ambivalent legal situation:* on the one hand, there are potential *autonomy gains* for the person affected resulting from the concept of capacity for consent; on the other hand, however, there is also a noticeable loss of *certainty of the law*—an ambivalence which should also be considered in the case of other "vulnerable" categories of persons.

Only in passing it should be noted that, though the concept of the capacity for consent may be of special importance in the context of medical law, it is also relevant in other contexts, either of a strictly personal nature or relating to personal rights—so to speak, with "personal rights in other respects".[17] This is true, for example, of the *right to informational self-determination* in the privacy law, which has given rise to extensive debate on the relevant problems of the capacity for consent as a legal concept, specifically in the case of minors.[18] A particularly pertinent example here would be the problems associated with "privacy protection for minors and media reporting".[19]

2.2.2 Decision-Making Level, Participation Level, Veto

The problems extend to individual issues which can only be mentioned in passing here. As a starting point, however, it can be noted that increasing consideration is given to the medically-related rights of minors, and thus their autonomous health-competence. This involves both decision-making and participation rights, especially in relation to custodial guardians. Between the exclusive decision-making rights of parents on the one hand and those of minors on the other, it is a matter of codecision rights for both. On the minors' side this also involves the "veto rights"[20] emphasized by the courts—rights, which in the secondary literature concerning the self-determination of those able to consent, are sometimes regarded as deficient.[21]

A stronger legal position is increasingly being granted to minors, even young children, beyond the decision-making level at the level of *participation and involvement* in the form of *information and consultation rights as well as rights to express their opinion.* In this sense, a noticeable increase in the involvement of these patients can be observed. And this is explicitly applicable at the informational level also in the case of *persons lacking the capacity for consent*, being emphasized just as much

[17] Ohly, *"Volenti non fit iniuria." Die Einwilligung im Privatrecht*, 2002, p. 55.

[18] Cf. the extensive discussion, with numerous references, in: Buchner, *Informationelle Selbstbestimmung im Privatrecht*, 2006, pp. 231 ff., pp. 236 ff., pp. 247 ff., pp. 274 ff.

[19] The title of Beater's article in *Juristenzeitung* 2013, p. 111.

[20] German Supreme Court, *Neue Juristische Wochenschrift* 2007, p. 217.

[21] Spickhoff, *Archiv für die civilistische Praxis* 208, 2008, p. 389: "a veto right only".

from the standpoint of child and adolescent psychiatry[22] as from the perspective of the law: "The capacity for consent and to be informed are by no means linked in such way that someone affected by a decision but lacking the capacity for consent would not have to be informed; on the contrary: in personal matters, people have a legitimate right to information even when they cannot make a decision (on their own)".[23] This also has to apply, correspondingly, to older people. The Federal Constitutional Court (in the context of compulsory treatment) has laid down the rule: "Even in the case of those without the capacity for consent, medical information on the intended treatment is not *a priori* dispensable," and this is true "independent of the question as to whether effective consent is attainable as a result of imparting the information. . . The information of the person concerned consistent with his ability to understand is therefore not superfluous".[24] Here the court speaks of a "wooing of consent through information",[25] thereby coining a remarkable phrase. The legislature that drafted the *Patients' Rights Law* reacted "at the last minute"[26] with § 630e V BGB, more thoroughly addressing patients lacking the capacity for consent—again, an age-independent regulation which was celebrated as "true progress".[27] A development of this kind in a specialized area of the law can be thought of as a way of concretizing and specifying the general development of a "medical information law" and as part of an overall "legal constitution for medical communication".[28]

Accordingly, it can be maintained that, although the well-being of the child and the right of parental care have traditionally occupied center stage, in recent times the personal rights and competencies of the child in conflicts involving medical decisions in various operating contexts have been gaining in importance. In summary, the *German Council of Ethics*' postulate regarding the increasing self-determination of children applies here:

> The older children become, the more autonomy they enjoy—an autonomy not merely granted by law, but also observable through their own capabilities . . . These days, children are seen as having rights and autonomous creative capabilities more so than in the past. Describing them mostly with reference to their limitations, and subjecting them completely to the will of their parents in upbringing and education, is generally frowned upon today.[29]

---

[22] Kölch, *Aufklärung bei klinischen Studien mit Kindern und Jugendlichen*, in: Wiese-mann/Dörries/Wolfslast/Simon (eds.), *Das Kind als Patient. Ethische Konflikte zwischen Kindeswohl und Kindeswille*, 2003, pp. 59 ff.

[23] Taupitz, Gutachten zum 63. *Deutscher Juristentag*, 2000, pp. A 59 ff.

[24] Federal Constitutional Court, *Neue Juristische Wochenschrift* 2011, p. 2113 (2116); more references on this in: Coester-Waltjen, *Medizinrecht* 2012, p. 554, Fn. 24.

[25] Federal Constitutional Court, *Neue Juristische Wochenschrift* 2011, p. 2113 (2117).

[26] Katzenmeier, *id.*, p. 38.

[27] Gleixner-Eberle, *id.*, p. 455.

[28] Damm, *Medizinisches Informationsrecht – Grundlagen und aktuelle Entwicklungen*, in: Stamm (ed.), *Fest-schrift für Helmut Rüßmann*, 2013, pp. 409 ff.

[29] Deutscher Ethikrat, *Demenz und Selbstbestimmung*, 2012, pp. 64 f.

2.3 *Age and Dementia*

2.3.1 Adults and Capacity for Consent

At the other end of the human life-cycle are the elderly, who are both similar to and different from the young in certain ways. Firstly we should pose the question: "At what age does one actually become 'old'?" This is related to an issue which surfaces in reference to another basic question of interest to us here: "the fundamental inquiry into the relationship between autonomy and heteronomy with advancing age".[30] There is, certainly, no "law of old age" to set any boundaries.[31] "'Old' people as a group can hardly be defined by rigid age-limits... Unlike children and adolescents, adults cannot be denied the capacity of self-determination merely by reason of age, even the most advanced age, especially not in a suitably categorical manner—stereotypically, as it were".[32]

To start with, though, there do also exist some more-or-less similar normative problems and structures, particularly with reference to self-determination and care. In this respect, normative parallels between the "long lives" of the elderly and the "short lives" of the young can be discerned. This is especially true in the context of age and dementia. The development of normative guidelines and principles for handling those in need of care and suffering from dementia presents a special challenge for the disciplines that deal with it, including legal theory and practice.[33] In the debate and rule-formulation relating to this issue, the relationship between self-determination and care is one of the fundamental problems. The concept of being able to understand and give consent also applies in principle to adults who, on account of illness or disability, are incapable of comprehending the significance of a medical or nursing procedure and making a decision on the matter. In this respect, it does not matter whether the party concerned possesses contractual competence. Consequently, persons with intellectual disabilities or mental disorders or suffering from senile dementia can thus be contractually incompetent, but despite that fact capable of consenting.[34] Beyond this fundamental accordance though, a few somewhat controversial distinctions can also be detected when carrying out a normative differentiation. From a legal standpoint, the following noteworthy principles have been formulated into a weighty statement:

---

[30] Citations found in: Spickhoff, *Archiv für die civilistische Praxis* 208, 2008, p. 347.

[31] Spickhoff, *Archiv für die civilistische Praxis* 208, 2008, p. 347, in reference to: Ganner, *Selbstbestimmung im Alter*, 2005, pp. 19 ff.

[32] Spickhoff, *Archiv für die civilistische Praxis* 208, 2008, p. 347.

[33] I have dealt extensively with this subject in: Damm, *Medizinrechtliche Grundprinzipien im Kontext von Pflege und Demenz – "Selbstbestimmung und Fürsorge"*, *Medizinrecht* 2010, pp. 451 ff.

[34] Jürgens, *Kritische Vierteljahresschrift für Gesetzgebung und Rechtsprechung* 1998, p. 34 (37).

> Adults with capacity for consent are—unlike minors with capacity for consent according to some (questionable) case law—competent to consent on their own to medical procedures. Adults capable of self-expression but not consent can legally refuse to consent, as long as no serious danger is imminent. The wishes of an adult without capacity for consent are equally binding regarding medically justifiable (further) treatment.[35]

Some of the difference, however, disappears if an autonomous capacity for decision-making is also adopted (*contra* the criticized case law) for minors with consent-capacity in applicable cases. This would give rise to a normative accordance between both minors and adults with capacity for consent by eliminating some "dubious unequal treatment".[36]

Rule-formation in this area can be pursued on various levels. Only two aspects are investigated in what follows: first, the debates within the profession concerning norms and standards; and second, the balancing act between care which limits the freedom and self-determination to be granted, using relevant case-law for examples.

2.3.2 Formulating Professional Norms

Regarding the first aspect of formulating professional norms for treatment and care standards, decisive importance is naturally accorded to the protective function favoring the persons concerned. In the field of care which is especially relevant here, there have been debates concerning quality-assurance and the setting of standards in recent times. This has also found expression in the diligent formulation of norms within the field—norms which aim at something variously described as "care-relevant standards" or "expert standards for care". Not coincidentally, the tension here between *care* and *self-determination* is center-stage. This is true, for example, of the "evidence-based guidelines for practice, the avoidance of measures that limit freedom in the professional care of the elderly",[37] and the "pilot-project for reducing the use of bodily restraints on dementia patients in nursing homes." The "Charter of Rights for People in Need of Care and Assistance" (2005) emphasizes in its very first article the self-determination of persons in need of care; only after that comes the protection of "body and mind".[38] The call for *Guidelines for Care* after the model of medical guidelines exemplifies this trend.[39] This refers to professional norms as a result of rule-formulation within the discipline, the significance of which for the practice of nursing and even more for legal practice has yet to be conclusively established. In this respect, we encounter basically the same problems as in the expanding field of medical professional norms in general. Their "origin and validity"

---

[35] Spickhoff, *Archiv für die civilistische Praxis* 208, 2008, p. 414.

[36] Spickhoff, *Archiv für die civilistische Praxis* 208, 2008, p. 389.

[37] From 2009, last retrieved on March 3, 2021; located at http://www.leitlinie-fem.de/download/LeitlinieFEM.pdf - Also covers liability-law related aspects, including relevant Federal Court of Justice case law (pp. 77f).

[38] Individual references in: Damm, *Medizinrecht* 2010, pp. 454 f., Fn. 29 ff.

[39] Klie, *PflegeRecht* 2008, p. 366 (374).

are still the subjects of ongoing debate, both in their own professional field as well as from a legal standpoint.[40]

2.3.3 The Judicial Balancing-Act Between Self-Determination and Restrictions on Freedom

In addition to these processes of norm-setting within the profession itself, there is also some important momentum in the case-law towards balancing self-determination and care with reference to restrictions of the freedom of persons in need of care and assistance. Even basic principles and rules governing care are put to the test in situations involving a conflict, and consequently also in the adjudication of legal conflicts. In this context, I will not explore the sometimes complex problems of social, care home and guardianship law, but simply point out the recent case law of the *Federal Court of Justice* which representatively mirrors the balancing act under discussion. We are referring to the court's rulings on nursing care from 2005, which have become known as the "Berlin case"[41] and the "Dresden case"[42] in the relevant literature.

By way of illustration, let us briefly outline the situation in the "Berlin case": *A woman was admitted to a nursing home in 1997 at the age of 85. She had already suffered a femoral neck fracture in 1994, forcing her to use a crutch. After another fall she had sustained a cranio-cerebral injury. She had very poor eyesight, occasionally became disoriented and was categorized as care level III. At the home she suffered another fall in 1998. The point at issue now involved another fall in 2001 which had occurred during the noon-break of the meanwhile 89 year old, leading to significant medical expenses.*

As in the "Dresden case," the plaintiff was the statutory health insurance company, which claimed damages from the owners of the care-home arising through subrogation of rights (§116 Para. 1 SGB X) in order to cover the medical expenses incurred. The plaintiff simply assumed that the care home was responsible for the injuries and would have to prove that they were not caused by a culpable violation on the part of the service personnel. Specifically, the home was accused of failing to strap down the patient during the noon-break or use bedrails. In the opinion of the plaintiff, other methods of fall-prevention should also have been considered, such as sensor-mattresses, photo-electric systems and hip protector briefs.[43]

Cases of this sort present us with very complex problems. In connection with my subject, I will only explore the tension between the *duties of protection and care* on

---

[40] Extensive treatment of this in: Damm, *Medizinrecht* 2010, pp. 454 f.; Damm, *Wie wirkt "Nichtrecht"? Genesis und Geltung privater Regeln am Beispiel medizinischer Professionsnormen*, *Zeitschrift für Rechtssoziologie* 2009, pp. 3 ff.

[41] Federal Court of Justice, *Neue Juristische Wochenschrift* 2005, p. 1937.

[42] Federal Court of Justice, *Neue Juristische Wochenschrift* 2005, p. 2613.

[43] Cf. the judgement review of: Dörr *PflegeRecht* 2006, p. 353.

the one hand, and the *self-determination* of the persons involved on the other. To start with the view of the Federal Court of Justice: "When residing in a home, the dignity, the interests and the needs of the residents are to be protected, and their independence, self-determination and self-responsibility are to be safeguarded and supported".[44] It should however be emphasized that the court also includes throughout "what is economically reasonable for a nursing home" in its evaluations. Consequently, nursing home owners and staff are "by no means justified in taking, or obligated to take, every conceivable precaution in order to avoid a fall under any circumstance. The paramount importance of the basic rights of the parties affected ... represent constitutional boundaries of appropriate protective measures".[45] For the nursing profession and the practice of law, as well as for the subject of this article, emphasis should be placed on the *reference to the individual case* by the court. Consequently, "it is impossible to determine categorically the specific content of the obligation to respect the personal dignity and freedom of an elderly, sick person on the one hand, and to protect their body and physical integrity on the other; rather, such a determination can be made only on the basis of a careful consideration of all the relevant circumstances of each individual case".[46]

To summarize, it is these two aspects which should be emphasized especially: first, the necessary balancing between safety and freedom, as well as between care and self-determination, is carried out on the basis of the individual case, countering the attempt of the health insurance filing suit to assume rather generally a breach of duty on the part of the nursing home owner and staff in the case of injuries resulting from a fall. Secondly, it should be noted that, as a result of its deliberations, the court arrived at a higher prioritization of the issues of self-determination and freedom of mobility, even in the case of patients suffering from the most severe forms of immobilization, disorientation and mental incapacitation.

An international comparison reveals that in other legal systems as well

> there has been a trend toward giving greater weight to autonomy in the conflict between the state's obligation to protect autonomy and to provide care. Against this background, measures requiring forced care are viewed with unease by the law. But here we cannot overlook the fact that care institutions, and the medical and nursing staff who work in them, are forced to confront some difficult choices involving the risk of liability on the one hand, and violating a patient's right to self-determination on the other.[47]

[44] Federal Court of Justice, *Neue Juristische Wochenschrift* 2005, p. 1937 (1938).

[45] Lang/Herkenhoff, *Neue Juristische Wochenschrift* 2005, p. 1906.

[46] Federal Court of Justice, *Neue Juristische Wochenschrift* 2005, p. 1937 (1938).

[47] So it is in Swiss law: Pärli, *Zwangsmaßnahmen in der Pflege, Allgemeine Juristische Praxis* 2011, p. 360 (369).

3 Special Areas of Medical Activity

Special areas of modern medicine, in which determining the appropriate ambits of protective care and possible self-determination pose serious legal problems, are representative and significant for the legal questions we are dealing with here. This is true of medical research, transplantation, and elective procedures such as cosmetic surgery and genetic testing. In these areas, problems of scope and boundary-setting for self-determination and the idea of a capacity to understand and consent play an important and sometimes controversial role. Here we can only offer some brief remarks on the subject, which, moreover, are related to only a few of the pertinent areas. We shall have to leave aside other important areas of medicine, such as the vital field of *reproductive medicine*.[48] It can be assumed, however, that the relevance of the problems presented here concerning self-determination and care in an increasing number of "specialty" fields is at the same time proof of the increasingly general significance of these problems and norms.

3.1 Research

The progress of the debate on the complex questions arising from the research on the young and the old can be summarized as follows: The situation of minors is receiving special scrutiny in medical-research law which has revealed two conflicting tendencies. On the one hand, there are reservations on the subject of including this category of people in medical research projects; on the other, there are indications that research and funding in the field of pediatric illnesses has intensified.[49] By way of contrast, the elderly have not received a comparable amount of attention from the research community, this corresponds to the fact that there is still no "law of old age".[50] The problem of *capacity for consent* is especially relevant for both age groups in this area as well.[51] Nevertheless, the identification of an age-dependent incapacity for consent presents us with special problems. And adequately involving and informing minors and the elderly is both a prerequisite and a problem at the same time. Thus, questions regarding the "participation of persons without capacity for consent in the decision-making process",[52] and informing

[48]Recent, extensive handling of this subject in: Neuner, *Das Recht auf reproduktive Selbstbestimmung, Archiv für die civilistische Praxis* 214, 2014, pp. 459 ff. Dealing specifically with questions relevant to our discussion here, such as the capacity for consent and self-determination of minors: Ohly, *id.*, pp. 306 ff., with further references.

[49]Taupitz, *Medizinrecht* 2012, p. 583, with reference to the EU's pediatric regulation.

[50]Taupitz, *Medizinrecht* 2012, p. 588, with reference to: Spickhoff, *Archiv für die civilistische Praxis* 208, 2008, p. 345, p. 347.

[51]For example: Taupitz, *Medizinrecht* 2012, pp. 584 f.

[52]More on this with further references in: Taupitz, *Medizinrecht* 2012, p. 583.

children and young people when conducting clinical studies[53] are also fundamental issues in this context (which have yet to be sufficiently clarified). Not coincidentally, pharmaceutical research is the main focus of interest in all of this.

3.2 Transplantation Medicine

Tellingly, in the legal provisions governing medical transplantation, both the regulatory concept of *capacity for consent* as well as that of fixed age-limits are contained in the body of standards. From the age of 16 on, minors can consent to *postmortal organ and tissue removal;* beginning at the age of fourteen, they can refuse permission for same (§ 2 II, 3 Transplantation Act [TPG]). For a *living-donor transplantation of an organ*, German law demands both that the person be an adult and capable of consent concurrently (§ 8 I No. 1a TPG). The legislature sought by this to exclude, for their own protection, the persons with intellectual or emotional disabilities or mental disorders from the possibility of donating their organs.[54] Even here, capacity for consent is not bound exclusively to an age of consent. The fixed age-limit of majority as an additional requirement is, however, supposed to secure legislative intent. In the secondary literature mention is made of the fact that establishing an individual capacity for consent because of possible pressure from the family can create considerable difficulties; while at the same time, an age-limit of majority affords the doctor in charge of the transplantation legal protection.[55]

Regarding the removal of bone marrow from minors, § 8a TPG focuses on the legal age of majority. In contrast, the rule on removing organs and tissue for transplant in § 8c TPG is based on capacity for consent; that is, whether the person in question "is in a position to appreciate the essence, meaning and import of the planned removal and to exercise their will accordingly" (§ 8c II TPG). If this is not the case, it is based on the informing and consent of a legal representative. The growing trend towards involvement that we mentioned before is also reflected in these regulatory contexts when a minor is to be informed by his/her doctor, "as far as this is possible given his/her age and level of psychological maturity." And a refusal by the minor of the intended removal or appropriation is to be "respected," without, however, specifying the consequences of a refusal (both regulations found in § 8a, sentence 1 No. 4 TPG).

---

[53] Kölch, *Aufklärung bei klinischen Studien mit Kindern und Jugendlichen*, in: Wiese-mann/Dörries/Wolfslast/Simon (eds.), *Das Kind als Patient. Ethische Konflikte zwischen Kindeswohl und Kindeswille*, 2003, pp. 59 ff.

[54] *BT-Drucks*. 13/4355, p. 20.

[55] Esser, in: Höfling (ed.), *Transplantationsgesetz, Kommentar*, 2003, § 8 margin num. 18.

3.3 *Elective Procedures and Cosmetic Surgery*

Serious problems also arise in the context of interest here when the subject of "elective surgery" is raised—especially with regard to aesthetic surgery. Here we are only addressing situations where there exists no medical indication for a procedure, as in the case of "cosmetic surgery." So in this case, in addition to the self-determination of the person in question, "an objective criterion of medical indication" is to be taken into consideration when assessing the situation.[56] A sizeable percentage of young people also undergo procedures of this sort.[57] It is therefore no wonder that questions regarding the scope and boundaries of self-determination for minors in such matters are also increasingly surfacing in problems handled by the legal system.[58] The relationship between the capacity for consent and autonomy of minors on the one hand, and the weight of parental care and decision-making competence on the other, can result in tension. When this occurs, a special need for protection in light of the not inconsiderable risks involved in such procedures when performed on minors is to be assumed.[59] In this context, we should also take into consideration the at least partly questionable concepts of "autonomy" in the area of medically non-indicated procedures. Intense debates on the issue are taking place regarding the extent to which market-interests, social control and media influence effectively overwhelm self-determination in such cases.[60]

3.4 *Genetic Testing*

Finally, as far as genetic diagnostics—especially predictive genetic testing—are concerned, problems related to *capacity for consent* play a role as well. In this context, we should mention the special legal regulations governing genetic testing on persons incapable of consent (§ 14 Genetic Diagnostics Act [GenDG]). The *Genetic Diagnostics Commission* has laid down an important guideline on genetic tests in

---

[56]Ohly, *id.*, p. 305.

[57]More on this with references in: Damm, *Medizinrechtliche Aspekte der Ästhetischen Chirurgie*, in: Lüttenberg/Ferrari (eds.), *Im Dienste der Schönheit? Interdisziplinäre Perspektiven auf die Ästhetische Chirurgie*, 2011, p. 207 (226).

[58]Extensive discussion of this subject in: Hennig, *Rechtliche Aspekte der ästhetischen Chirurgie bei Minderjährigen. Tattoos, Piercings, Schönheitsoperationen. Zur rechtlichen Problematik nicht indizierter Eingriffe bei Minderjährigen*, 2012.

[59]Hennig, *id.*, p. 250 f.

[60]The counter-point, "autonomous choice, or 'social subjugation'," is trenchantly formulated in: Herrmann, *Schönheitsideal und medizinische Körpermanipulation. Invasive Selbstgestaltung als Ausdruck autonomer Entscheidung oder ‚sozialer Unterwerfung'?, Ethik in der Medizin* 2006, p. 71.

such cases,[61] dealing with limits of admissibility and rules for involving subjects. As a precondition for involving a person incapable of consent, the test must be "explained to him/her in the most appropriate way possible," and the person must not "object" to the test (§ 14 I Num. 2 GenDG). As for genetic testing involving blood relations, some hitherto unheard of and dramatic cases have come before the courts recently which have presented the judiciary with considerable problems, and precisely in the area of capacity for consent among minors. In one such case involving the hereditary and incurable *Huntington's disease*, the district court held that the capacity for consent of a sixteen-year-old "at risk" to a genetic test "posed no problem." The regional court of appeals, however, followed a diametrically opposed line of reasoning in the case. In the court's view, the usual civil-law categories for determining capacity for consent must be applied "restrictively" in view of the "complexity" of genetic testing results. Referring to the afore-mentioned guideline from the Genetic Diagnostics Commission governing genetic testing on persons incapable of consent, the court assumed that while the capacity for consent "may" in principle arise even before a person attains majority, it would be subject to "strict requirements".[62]

In the area of *dementia*, predictive diagnostics is also associated with particular problems.[63] This is especially true with regard to unpreventable disorders, which are not causally treatable. In cases of *early diagnosis*, it must be assumed that the subject is (still) in possession of the requisite *capacity to understand and consent*. This has implications for what is, in this area as well, the critical issue of determining the scope of autonomous decisions, especially in connection with prediction, prevention and responsibility. Complex problems—legal ones, too—arise out of the many and various types of diseases. This definitely holds true for the distinction between the main group of "sporadic" disorders and the numerically smaller, yet in many respects important group of genetic disorders. Only the latter group is regulated by the *Genetic Diagnostics Law*—if we are referring here to the law's immediate area of application, at any rate. The question as to whether the application of important basic

[61] Gendiagnostik-Kommission, *"Richtlinie zur genetischen Untersuchung bei nicht-einwilligungsfähigen Personen nach § 14 in Verbindung mit § 23 Abs. 2 Nr. 1c GenDG", Bundesgesundheitsblatt – Gesundheitsforschung – Gesundheitsschutz* 2011, pp. 1257 ff.

[62] OLG Koblenz *Medizinrecht* 2014, p. 168; more extensive treatment of this subject complete with citations in: Damm, *Medizinrecht* 2014, p. 139; and previously: Damm, *Medizinrecht* 2012, p. 705; the appellate decision has now been issued, but the reasoning, however, is not very enlightening: BGH *Juristenzeitung* 2014, p. 898, with commentary from: Katzenmeier/Voigt, *Juristenzeitung* 2014, p. 900; BGH *Zeitschrift für das gesamte Familienrecht* 2014, p. 1288, with commentary from: Spickhoff, *Zeitschrift für das gesamte Familienrecht* 2014, p. 1291.

[63] Much more on this and on what follows in: Damm, *Prädiktive Diagnostik und Demenz. Rechtliche Grundprobleme und medizinische Optionen, GesundheitRecht* 2013, pp. 385 ff.

principles and regulatory precepts found in the "Genetic Diagnostics Act as regulatory model" could also be considered for the field of non-genetic predictive science will not be further entertained here.[64]

Additionally, a new controversy has developed in the field of genetic diagnostics around the very recent Genetic Diagnostics Act, especially with regard to the tension between *autonomy and care.* The German *science academies* have criticized the act on the grounds that it wrongly weights the right of autonomy *vis-à-vis* the medical duty of care.[65] This criticism refers to the relationship between informational self-determination, confidentiality and the duty of care, and the regulatory concepts in § 10 III, 4 und § 11 III of the GenDG. Regarding the consequences for third parties when conducting genetic tests within a family, the science academies plead for a moderating of confidentiality with respect to the person examined and his/her right of informational self-determination, while demanding a strengthening of the duty of care with respect to other family members who are possibly risk cases, genetically speaking. The changes proposed by the academies reflect an accentuation of the relationship between (informational) self-determination and duty of care that differs from the basic premises of medical law and ethics up till now, even if only in the special case of genetic diagnostics.[66]

4 Problems and Perspectives of Norm formulation

This article has dealt with the conditions and boundaries of self-determination and care, with a focus on those who are especially at risk or "vulnerable". In conclusion, some fundamental problems involving norm formulation should be particularly emphasized. These observations are to be oriented around the following pairs of keywords: *normativity and facticity* of deficient or "imperfect autonomy"[67] and exceptional vulnerability; *individualizing or typifying* when determining the target-group of legal self-determination postulates and policies protecting care; and finally, *the goals of protection and legal rights* and to a certain extent, the relationship between *self-determination and care revisited.*

---

[64] A more detailed treatment in: Damm, *Prädiktive Diagnostik und Demenz, GesundheitRecht* 2013, p. 387.

[65] Nationale Akademie der Wissenschaften Leopoldina/acatech-Deutsche Akademie der Technikwissenschaften/Berlin-Brandenburgische Akademie der Wissenschaften, *Prädiktive genetische Diagnostik als Instrument der Krankheitsprävention*, 2010.

[66] More on this in: Damm *Medizinrecht* 2014, p. 143 f.

[67] More in: Damm, *Imperfekte Autonomie und Neopaternalismus. Medizinrechtliche Probleme der Selbstbestim-mung in der modernen Medizin, Medizinrecht* 2002, p. 375; also reprinted in: Robertson (ed.), *Der perfekte Mensch. Genforschung zwischen Wahn und Wirklichkeit*, 2003, pp. 153 ff.

4.1 Normativity and Facticity

Our discussion here also raises the question: On which knowledge-base is the discourse on the capability of self-determination, "health competence" and the need of care of the persons and populations concerned being conducted? In other words, what about the empirical evidence of vulnerability in general, and especially the facticity of capacity for consent over the course of a lifetime? General references to supposed evidence of "exceptional need for protection" simply will not suffice in this case. It is much more precisely a matter of knowing the scope and boundaries of *behavioral dispositions, competencies and chances for the young and old to participate* in medical, care-oriented and nursing-related situations. Therefore, especially also from a legal point of view, the recent efforts gaining momentum in various specialties and across disciplines concerning the *empirical validity* of the treatment of children and adolescents, as well as the elderly and those suffering from dementia are significant and welcome. Thus, the discussion of the "child as patient"[68] includes methodological and empirical works on "children's capacity for self-determination in medicine",[69] and on "the establishment of capacity for consent in children".[70] In the field of *psychiatry* there are also reports of extensive research into ascertaining the capacity for consent.[71] Turning to *dementia*, the first discursive contacts between medicine and law have been made in light of the state of research in that field. This is true, for example, of the relevance (including legal relevance) of the afore-mentioned distinction between genetically-conditioned Alzheimer's and the so-called sporadic variety, and it is also true generally of knowledge relating to the *genetics and epigenetics of dementia*.[72]

And so the entire nexus of *prediction, prevention and responsibility* is touched upon, and also with an eye to questions about the capacity to understand and consent in the young and the elderly. Once again, let our discussion of genetic diagnostics and of the meaning of capacity for consent be pointed out in this regard. All in all, what we have here in this context is a legal perspective on knowledge-creating scientific disciplines and a focus on the problem that we could, following the model of "evidence-based medicine," characterize as *evidence-based norm formulation,* or, taking our cue from a phrase coined recently, as "evidence-based jurisprudence".[73]

---

[68] Wiesemann/Dörries/Wolfslast/Simon (eds.), *id.*

[69] Alderson, *Die Autonomie des Kindes – über die Selbstbestimmungsfähigkeit von Kindern in der Medizin*, in: Wiesemann/Dörries/Wolfslast/Simon (eds.), *id.*, pp. 28 ff.

[70] Vollmann, *Konzeptionelle und methodische Fragen bei der Feststellung der Einwilligungsfähigkeit bei Kindern*, in: Wiesemann/Dörries/Wolfslast/Simon (eds.), *id.*, pp. 48 ff.

[71] Vollmann, *Einwilligungsfähigkeit als relationales Konzept. Klinische Praxis und medizinethische Analyse*, *Nervenarzt* 2000, p. 709 (710 f.).

[72] More extensive reading on the subject with references: Damm, *GesundheitRecht* 2013, p. 385, pp. 387 ff.

[73] In the very different legal field of corporate law, but also referring to the model of "evidence-based medicine": Hanjo Hamann, *Evidenzbasierte Jurisprudenz. Methoden der empirischen Forschung und ihr Erkenntniswert für das Recht am Beispiel des Gesellschaftsrechts*, 2014.

"Evidence-based law" now also takes its place (in the form of a question) as the title of a problem of health and social law.[74]

4.2 Individualizing or Typifying

When defining the target-groups of legal stipulations for self-determination and protective policies, one can pursue various types of normative strategies, ranging from individualization to typification; that is, attention will be directed more or less strongly at either *persons or populations*, or at *the specification or generalization of the situational context.* In each case, the consequences can be significant. Among other things, this applies to the notorious—in fact, classic—problem of reconciling *justice in a particular case* with *certainty of the law.* On the one hand, we have the specifying individual reference to a (legal) norm intended to ensure greater accuracy regarding the specific individual when deciding in a particular case between the right of autonomy and the need for protection; on the other hand, a group-specific population reference can, with its generalizing approach, offer more certainty in decision-making as well as legal consistency in cases of doubt. However, it can also result in a more-or-less faulty decision in a particular case of need for protection versus capacity for self-determination.

In this context we should also point out the numerous statutory provisions which are based on fixed age-categories in the interests of legal consistency—categories mostly relating to young people.[75] Considering this, and the fact that the legislature has also repeatedly ascribed "partial competence" to minors under 16, a "sufficient inductive basis" is seen for a "capacity for consent beginning in principle at the age of 16".[76] A "general exclusive competence" such as this, however, cannot apply from the age of 16 without restrictions, so in cases of extraordinary complexity, the legislature also provided for joint-consent, including the minor of age and his/her legal representatives.[77] A "general principle" has been derived from the provisions in question, according to which "cumulative consent is required in cases involving especially risky procedures or forms of treatment".[78]

On the subject of the elderly, things are more complicated. Let it be pointed out once again that

---

[74] Augsberg, *Evidence-based Law im Sozial- und Gesundheitsrecht? Chancen und Grenzen eines epistemologi-schen Modells, Vortrag auf der Tagung zu "Wissensgenerierung und –verarbeitung im Gesundheits- und Sozial-recht"*; workshop on the occasion of the 65th birthday of Friedhelm Hase, Bremen, 5. März 2015.

[75] Evidence for this in: Wolf/Neuner, *id.*, p. 129.

[76] Wolf/Neuner, *id.*, p. 129.

[77] Wolf/Neuner, *id.*, p. 129, with references to medical transplantation and clinical trials of pharmaceuticals and medical devices, among other things.

[78] Wolf/Neuner, *id.*, p. 129.

> the category of the 'the elderly' can hardly be defined by means of rigid age-boundaries . . . Unlike children and adolescents, adults cannot be denied the capacity for self-determination by reason of old—even the oldest—age *per se* and especially not in a comparably generalized manner, i.e., in a quasi-categorical way . . . The German legal system is not the only one that assigns to each person as a free being, irrespective of age, the capacity for self-determination on an equal basis after leaving their youth behind.[79]

Apart from that, the normative question of individualization versus typification is also partly determined in each case by the category of activity involved. Thus, "the further one moves away from property-law questions and in the direction of subjects related to personal rights, the more the establishment of legal norms is to be guided by individual situations. The fine-tuning necessary for this circumscribes the possibilities for formulating generalized rules in the sense of legally consistent, 'one-size-fits-all' solutions".[80] This tailoring of the solution to the respective category of legally protected rights, whether personal or proprietary, is fundamentally deserving of approval and, with respect to the questions dealt with here, especially accentuated by the emphasis on a "*preferential weighting* of the right of self-determination *vis-à-vis* the protection of transactions".[81] In the tension that exists between individualization and typification when establishing norms, a distinctly normative orientation towards the right of self-determination thus tends to assert itself over, the pragmatic orientation towards legal certainty.

Corresponding to this is the observation that, in regards to relevant legally protected rights of a strictly personal nature, "transactional protection must, as a general rule, yield to the protection of minors".[82] And ultimately, the relevance of the transactional protection issue is also qualified by the consideration that, especially in the field of medicine, legal consistency can even in practice be attained only to a very limited extent by establishing age categories.[83]

4.3 *Protective Purposes and Legal Rights: Autonomy and Care Revisited*

The relationship between self-determination and care has recently once again, and in a somewhat different way, attracted some interdisciplinary attention as well. This does not only relate to the tendency to attach more importance to the issue of self-determination for people at either end of the life-cycle: This applies equally to the (co)decision-making levels, and especially to the rights of involvement and participation.

[79] All citations in: Spickhoff, *Archiv für die civilistische Praxis* 208, 2008, p. 347.

[80] Spickhoff, *Archiv für die civilistische Praxis* 208, 2008, p. 413.

[81] Spickhoff, *Archiv für die civilistische Praxis* 208, 2008, p. 355 [emphasis mine].

[82] Coester-Waltjen, *Medizinrecht* 2012, p. 558.

[83] More detailed treatment in: Coester-Waltjen, *Medizinrecht* 2012, p. 558.

More important still is the special emphasis on a *mutual definition of scope* for both legal positions. In this respect, it is about norm concepts which firmly understand self-determination and care as being in a relationship of *normative interdependency* and mutual improvement, instead of a relationship of *alternativeness without alternatives*. The postulates in question aim at using care, for its part, as an instrument for supporting and "facilitating self-determination".[84] Consequently, "the exceptional need for protection on the part of vulnerable persons extends especially to the recognition of patient autonomy ... Hence, respect for their autonomy requires greater attentiveness, effort and forbearance than in the case of other patients".[85] Not only is even a qualified potential for self-determination therefore something worth protecting for the person concerned, but self-determination itself is actually a *goal of care*.[86]

5 Conclusion

In summary, let it once again be emphasized that the special normative problems of particularly vulnerable persons at the beginning and the end of their lives pose special problems for the establishment of norms. This is not least a matter of the compatibility of a generalization of norm formulation with the context-specifics of norm application. Thus, not coincidentally, the German Ethics Council, in its policy brief on *Dementia and Self-determination*, stresses the importance of "basic rules which are valid for virtually all of the—very different—fields of application".[87] Hence: universal "validity, but also differing emphasis on these basic principles when considering individual groups of persons affected".[88]

Against this backdrop, there is good reason to continue working on a new calibration of self-determination and care, not least on an understanding of care that also encompasses support for self-determination, even if limited for the persons concerned. In this respect, it is a matter of *care for self-determination*. Amidst all these considerations it becomes clear to what extent medical law, as the law of persons of particularly vulnerable people, represents not only sections of the legal system, but also a touchstone of the legal culture as it affects society.

---

[84] German Ethics Council, *Demenz und Selbstbestimmung*, 2012, pp. 46 ff. (50); similarly: Alderson, *id.*, pp. 28 ff.

[85] Birnbacher, *Medizinrecht* 2013, p. 565.

[86] Cf. also in this context the concept of "capacity for consent as relational model" in: Vollmann, *Nervenarzt* 2000, p. 709.

[87] German Ethics Council, *Demenz und Selbstbestimmung*, 2012, p. 63.

[88] German Ethics Council, *Demenz und Selbstbestimmung*, 2012, p. 64.

References

Alderson, P. 2003. Die Autonomie des Kindes – über die Selbstbestimmungsfähigkeit von Kindern in der Medizin [The autonomy of the child – on childrens' capacity of self-determination in medicine]. In *Das Kind als Patient. Ethische Konflikte zwischen Kindeswohl und Kindeswille [The child as patient. Ethical conflicts between child welfare and child volition]*, eds. C. Wiesemann, A. Dörries, G. Wolfslast, and A. Simon, 28–47. Frankfurt am Main: Campus Verlag.

Augsberg, I. 2015. Evidence-based Law im Sozial- und Gesundheitsrecht? Chancen und Grenzen eines epistemologischen Modells, *Vortrag auf der Tagung zu „Wissensgenerierung und –verarbeitung im Gesundheits- und Sozialrecht"* [Evidence-based law in social and health law? Opportunities and limits of an epistemological model. *Lecture at the conference "Generating and processing knowledge in health and social law"]. Workshop on the occasion of the 65th birthday of Friedhelm Hase, 5. März 2015.* Bremen: Mohr Siebeck.

Beater, A. 2013. Persönlichkeitsschutz Minderjähriger und mediale Berichterstattung [Privacy protection for minors and media reporting]. *JuristenZeitung* 68 (3): 111–120.

Birnbacher, D. 2012. Vulnerabilität und Patientenautonomie – Anmerkungen aus medizinethischer Sicht [Vulnerability and patient autonomy – The medical-ethical perspective]. *Medizinrecht* 30 (9): 560–565.

Buchner, B. 2006. Informationelle Selbstbestimmung im Privatrecht [Informational self-determination in private law]. *Jus Privatum* 114. Tübingen: Mohr Siebeck.

Coester-Waltjen, D. 2012. Reichweite und Grenzen der Patientenautonomie von Jungen und Alten – ein Vergleich [Scope and limits of young and old patients' autonomy – a comparison]. *Medizinrecht* 30 (9): 553–560.

Damm, R. 2002. Imperfekte Autonomie und Neopaternalismus. Medizinrechtliche Probleme der Selbstbestimmung in der modernen Medizin [Imperfect autonomy and neopaternalism. Medical law problems of self-determination in modern medicine]. *Medizinrecht* 20 (8): 375–387.

Damm, R. 2009. Wie wirkt "Nichtrecht"? Genesis und Geltung privater Regeln am Beispiel medizinischer Professionsnormen [How does "No-Law" work? Genesis and validity of private rules using the example of medical professional standards]. *Zeitschrift für Rechtssoziologie* 30 (1): 3–22.

Damm, R. 2010. Medizinrechtliche Grundprinzipien im Kontext von Pflege und Demenz – "Selbstbestimmung und Fürsorge". [Rationales in medical law concerning care and dementia – "Self-determination and care"] *Medizinrecht* 28 (7): 451-463.

Damm, R. 2011. Medizinrechtliche Aspekte der Ästhetischen Chirurgie. Normstrukturen, Regelungsprobleme und Steuerungsebenen [Medical law aspects of aesthetic surgery. Norm structures, regulatory problems and control levels]. In *Im Dienste der Schönheit? Interdisziplinäre Perspektiven auf die Ästhetische Chirurgie [In the service of beauty? Interdisciplinary perspectives on aesthetic surgery]*, eds. B. Lüttenberg, A. Ferrari, and J. S. Ach, 207–246. Münster: Lit Verlag.

Damm, R. 2012. Prädikative Gendiagnostik im Familienverband und Haftungsrecht [Predictive genetic diagnostics within the family unit and liability law]. *Medizinrecht* 30 (11): 705-710.

Damm, R. 2013a. Medizinisches Informationsrecht – Grundlagen und aktuelle Entwicklungen [Medical information clauses – basics and current developments]. In *Festschrift für Helmut Rüßmann [Festschrift for Helmut Rüßmann]*, ed. J. Stamm, 409–429. Saarbrücken: juris GmbH.

Damm, R. 2013b. Prädiktive Diagnostik und Demenz: Rechtliche Grundprobleme und medizinische Optionen [Predictive diagnostics and dementia: Basic legal problems and medical options]. *GesundheitsRecht* 12 (7): 385–399.

Damm, R. 2014. Prädikative Gendiagnostik, Familienverband und Haftungsrecht [Predictive genetic diagnostics, family unit and liability law]. *Medizinrecht* 32 (3): 139–147.

Dörr, C. 2006. Die Pflegeurteile des Bundesgerichtshofs. (Zugleich Anmerkung zu BGH, U. v. 28.04.2005 - III ZR 399/04 - und Anmerkung zu BGH, U. v. 14.07.2005 - III ZR 391/04) [Care verdicts of Federal Court of Justice. (Commentary on BGH, U. v. 28.04.2005 - III ZR 399/04 – and Commentary on BGH, U. v. 14.07.2005 - III ZR 391/04]. *PflegeRecht* 31 (8): 353.

Ellenberger, J. 2014. Teil 1. Geschäftsfähigkeit [Legal capacity]. In *Bürgerliches Gesetzbuch [German Civil Code]* 73rd ed., eds. O. Palandt, 83-92. München: C. H. Beck.

Ganner, M. 2005. *Selbstbestimmung im Alter: Privatautonomie für alte und pflegebedürftige Menschen in Österreich und Deutschland [Self-determination in old age: Private autonomy for old people and people in need of care in Austria and Germany]*. New York, Wien: Springer Verlag.

Gendiagnostik-Kommission am Robert Koch-Institut. 2011. Richtlinie zur genetischen Untersuchung bei nicht-einwilligungsfähigen Personen nach § 14 in Verbindung mit § 23 Abs. 2 Nr. 1c GenDG [Guideline for genetic testing of persons not able to give consent according to § 14 in connection with § 23 Abs. 2 Nr. 1c GenDG]. *Bundesgesundheitsblatt – Gesundheitsforschung – Gesundheitsschutz* 11: 1257–1261.

Gleixner-Eberle, E. 2014. *Die Einwilligung in die medizinische Behandlung Minderjähriger. Eine arztrechtliche Untersuchung im Rechtsvergleich mit Österreich und der Schweiz sowie mit Blick auf das Internationale Privat- und Strafrecht [Consent in medical treatment of minors. An examination of medical law in the context of Austrian and Swiss law and with reference to international private and criminal law]*. Berlin, Heidelberg: Springer Verlag.

German Ethics Council. 2012. Demenz und Selbstbestimmung [Dementia and self-determination]. Berlin.

Hamann, H. 2014. Evidenzbasierte Jurisprudenz. Methoden der empirischen Forschung und ihr Erkenntniswert für das Recht am Beispiel des Gesellschaftsrechts [Evidence Based Jurisprudence. Methods and Epistemic Value of Empirical Research in Law, with Examples From Corporate Law]. *Grundlagen der Rechtswissenschaft* 23. Tübingen: Mohr Siebeck.

Hennig, L. 2012. Rechtliche Aspekte der ästhetischen Chirurgie bei Minderjährigen. Tattoos, Piercings, Schönheitsoperationen: Zur rechtlichen Problematik nicht indizierter Eingriffe bei Minderjährigen [Legal aspects of cosmetic surgery for minors. Tattoos, piercings, cosmetic surgery: On legal problems of non-indicated surgical procedures on minors]. *Hallesche Schriften zum Recht* 31. Halle: Universitätsverlag Halle-Wittenberg.

Herrmann, B. 2006. Schönheitsideal und medizinische Körpermanipulation. Invasive Selbstgestaltung als Ausdruck autonomer Entscheidung oder 'sozialer Unterwerfung'? [Beauty ideal and medical body manipulation. Invasive self-design as an expression of autonomous decision or "social submission"?] *Ethik in der Medizin* 18 (1): 71–80.

Hollerbach, A. 1996. *Selbstbestimmung im Recht [Self-determination in law]*. Sitzungsberichte der Heidelberger Akademie der Wissenschaften. Philosophisch-historische Klasse 2. Heidelberg: Universitätsverlag C. Winter.

Höfling, W., D. Esser, G. Feuerstein, W. F. Haupt, D. Henne-Bruns, H.-J. Kaatsch, H. Lang, S. Rixen, and J. in der Schmitten. 2003. *Transplantationsgesetz: Kommentar [Transplantation Act: Commentary]*. Berliner Kommentare 2. Berlin: Erich Schmidt Verlag.

Jürgens, A. 1998. Fremdnützige Forschung an einwilligungsunfähigen Personen nach deutschem Recht und nach dem Menschenrechtsübereinkommen für Biomedizin [Research for the benefit of outsiders on persons unable to give consent under German law and under the Convention on Human Rights in Biomedicine]. *Kritische Vierteljahresschrift für Gesetzgebung und Rechtswissenschaft* 81 (1): 34–51.

Katzenmeier, C. 2014. Patientenrechte und Arzthaftung, in Karlsruher Forum 2013 [Patient rights and medical liability]. *Schriftenreihe der Zeitschrift Versicherungsrecht* 52: 5–82.

Katzenmeier, C., and T. Voigt. 2014. Anmerkung [Commentary]. *JuristenZeitung (JZ)* 69 (18): 900–902.

Klie, T. 2008. Förderung von Mobilität und Sicherheit bei Menschen mit demenziellen Einschränkungen in stationären Einrichtungen und die Debatte um die "Aufsichtspflicht" [Promoting mobility and safety for people impaired by dementia in residential facilities and the "supervision" debate]. *PflegeRecht* 12 (8): 366–374.

Kölch, M. 2003. Aufklärung bei klinischen Studien mit Kindern und Jugendlichen [Counseling in clinical studies with children and adolescents]. In *Das Kind als Patient. Ethische Konflikte zwischen Kindeswohl und Kindeswille [The child as patient. Ethical conflicts between child welfare and child volition]*, eds. C. Wiesemann, A. Dörries, G. Wolfslast, and A. Simon, 59–71. Frankfurt am Main: Campus Verlag.

Lang, H., and M. Herkenhoff. 2005. Zur Rechtsprechung – Persönlichkeitsrechte und Menschenwürde im Alten- oder Pflegeheim [On case law – Personal rights and human dignity in retirement or nursing homes]. *Neue Juristische Wochenschrift* 58 (27): 1905–1906.

Nationale Akademie der Wissenschaften Leopoldina, acatech - Deutsche Akademie der Technikwissenschaften, and Berlin-Brandenburgische Akademie der Wissenschaften. 2010. *Stellungnahme. Prädiktive genetische Diagnostik als Instrument der Krankheitsprävention [Statement. Predictive Genetic Diagnostics as an instrument for disease prevention].* http://www.acatech.de/de/projekte/abgeschlossene-projekte/praediktive-genetische-diagnostik/print.html?type=98&cHash=938834059ec70796a5a560f0530eb73d. Accessed March 3, 2021.

Neuner, J. 2014. Das Recht auf reproduktive Selbstbestimmung. [The Right of Self-Determined Reproduction] *Archiv für die civilistische Praxis* 214: 459-510

Ohly, A. 2002. *"Volenti non fit iniuria" – die Einwilligung im Privatrecht ["Volenti non fit iniuria" – Consent in Private Law].* Jus Privatum 73. Tübingen: Mohr Siebeck.

Pärli, K. 2011. Zwangsmaßnahmen in der Pflege [Coercive measures in nursing care]. *Allgemeine Juristische Praxis* 3: 360–370.

Robertson, C. Y. 2003. *Der perfekte Mensch. Genforschung zwischen Wahn und Wirklichkeit [The perfect human. Genetic research between delusion and reality].* Schriften des Instituts für Angewandte Kulturwissenschaft der Universität Karlsruhe (TH) 8. Karlsruhe: Nomos Kulturwissenschaft.

Spickhoff, A. 2008. Autonomie und Heteronomie im Alter [Autonomy and heteronomy in old age]. *Archiv für die civilistische Praxis* 208: 345–415.

Spickhoff, A. 2014. Anmerkung zum Urteil des BGH v. 20.05.2014 (VI ZR 381/13 – Psychische Schäden durch Information über mögliche Erbkrankheit eigener Kinder [Commentary on the BGH decision of May 20, 2014 (VI ZR 381/13 - Psychological damage caused by receiving information about possible hereditary disease of own children]. *Zeitschrift für das gesamte Familienrecht* 1291: 1288.

Taupitz, J. 2000. Empfehlen sich zivilrechtliche Regelungen zur Absicherung der Patientenautonomie am Ende des Lebens? [Can civil law regulations be recommended to safeguard patient autonomy at the end of life?]. Gutachten A zum 63. Deutschen Juristentag Leipzig 2000. München: C.H. Beck.

Taupitz, J. 2012. Medizinische Forschung an jungen und alten Patienten [Medical research on young and old patients]. *Medizinrecht* 30 (9): 583–588.

Vollmann, J. 2000. Einwilligungsfähigkeit als relationales Modell. Klinische Praxis und medizinethische Analyse [Consent as relational model. Clinical practice and medical ethical analysis]. *Der Nervenarzt* 71 (9): 709–710. https://doi.org/10.1007/s001150050654.

Vollmann, J. 2003. Konzeptionelle und methodische Fragen bei der Feststellung der Einwilligungsfähigkeit bei Kindern [Conceptual and methodological questions in determining the ability to consent in children]. In *Das Kind als Patient. Ethische Konflikte zwischen Kindeswohl und Kindeswille [The child as a patient. Ethical conflicts between child welfare and child volition]*, eds. C. Wiesemann, A. Dörries, G. Wolfslast, and A. Simon, 7: 48–58. Frankfurt am Main: Campus Verlag.

Weidenkaff, W. 2014. Untertitel 2. Behandlungsvertrag. (§§ 630a-630h) [Subtitle 2. Treatment contract. (§§ 630a-630h)]. In: *Bürgerliches Gesetzbuch [German Civil Code]* 73rd ed., ed.. Palandt, O.,1009-1028. München: C. H. Beck.

Wolf, M., and J. Neuner. 2012. *Allgemeiner Teil des Bürgerlichen Rechts [General part of German Civil Law].* 10th ed. München: C.H. Beck Verlag.

The Extra Years: Creating More Opportunities for Women and Men by Redistributing (Working) Time

Jutta Allmendinger and Ellen von den Driesch

1 On the Labor Market Status of Women and Men

When it comes to gender equity, Germany still has a long way to go. Let's look at some facts. Although German women now outperform men in terms of obtaining a university entrance qualification (*Abitur*), starting university and actually finishing their degree, they are still much less likely than men to be part of the workforce, let alone work in a senior position. It is certainly true that more and more women are now integrated into the labor market; not least because, as well-trained workers, they are urgently needed to counter the impending skills shortage. Accordingly, the female employment rate increased significantly between 2005 and 2015, from 67 to 73%. Over the same period, the male employment rate increased only marginally, from 80 to 82% (cf. Bundesagentur für Arbeit 2017). In turn, the male/female employment gap is still at 9 percentage points.

Moreover, these employment rates gloss over some substantial differences. If women do work, they mostly work part time. This is especially the case for women with children. As shown in Fig. 1, the proportion of women in part-time employment rose from 19 to 31 percent between 1996 and 2016. The majority of them work in marginal part-time employment, that is, fewer than 15 h per week. By contrast, the proportion of women who worked in standard employment (i.e., those working in permanent full-time positions) was 29% in 2016. Male employment has seen a

J. Allmendinger
Wissenschaftszentrum Berlin für Sozialforschung, Berlin, Germany
e-mail: jutta.allmendinger@wzb.eu

E. von den Driesch (✉)
Wissenschaftszentrum Berlin für Sozialforschung, Berlin, Germany

Bundesinstitut für Bevölkerungsforschung, Wiesbaden, Germany
e-mail: ellen.driesch@wzb.eu

B. Schmitz-Luhn, C. Woopen (eds.), *Justice over the Course of Life*, Schriften zu Gesundheit und Gesellschaft - Studies on Health and Society 1,
https://doi.org/10.1007/978-3-030-86449-1_8

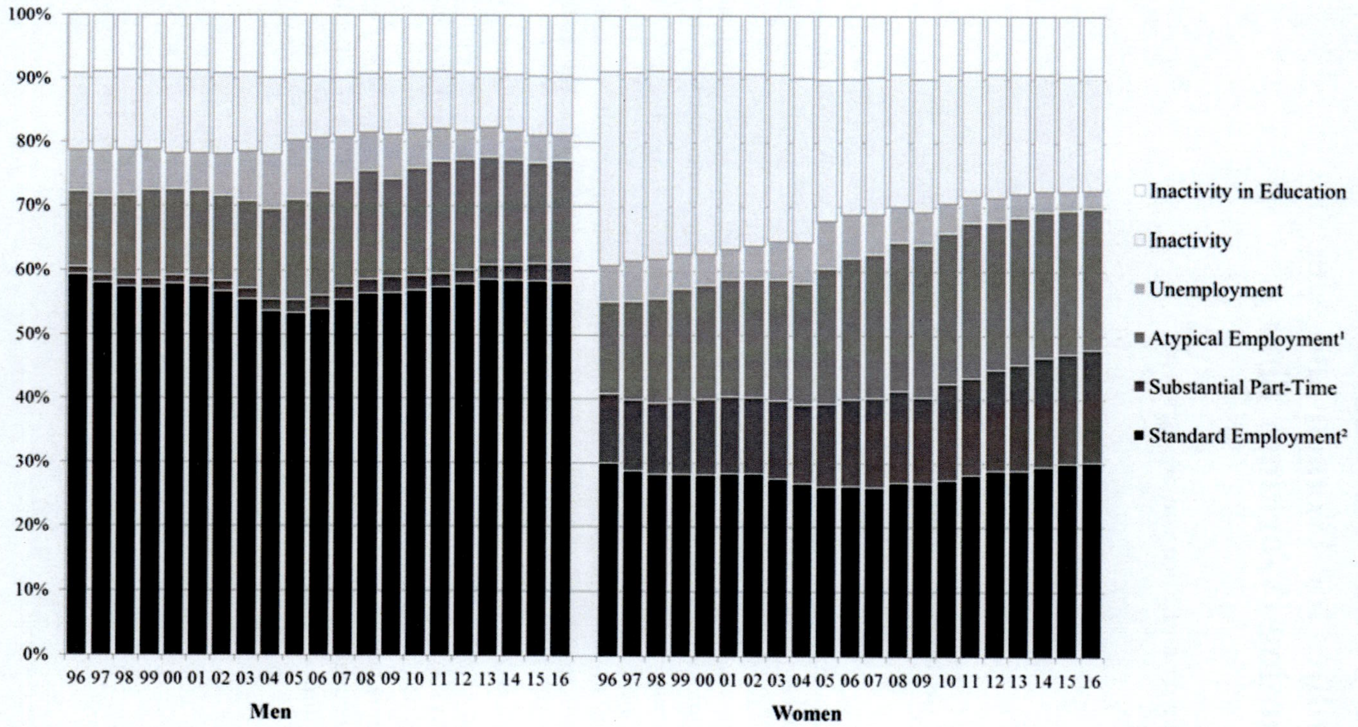

Fig. 1 Employment in Germany by gender, 1996–2016 (cf. Allmendinger et al. 2013b, figure updated by Stefan Stuth et al. 2018). Comment: In the above Fig. 1, persons are considered to be employed if they are in private or public employment or self-employed with a minimum workload of 1 h per week, receiving a wage, salary, or some other form of monetary compensation for their work. Persons are considered to be *unemployed* if they are not working but actively looking for work, if they are available in the labor market or starting a new job within the next 3 months. Economically *inactive* persons are those who are neither employed nor unemployed. Inactive persons who are engaged in continuing education and professional development are assigned to the *inactive in education*

category. The group of persons in *atypical employment* consists of *self-employed persons* without employees, persons in *marginal part-time employment* (fewer than 20 h), and persons in *temporary employment* working on a limited-term contract. (Here, a distinction is made between temporary full-time employment (35 and more hours/week) and temporary part-time employment (fewer than 35 h/week).) *Substantial part-time employment* refers to a type of employment that consists of more than 20 but fewer than 35 h per week. *Standard employment* refers to dependent employment of at least 35 h per week (full time) on a permanent contract (cf. Allmendinger et al. 2013b, figure updated by Stefan Stuth et al. 2018). [1]Atypical employment includes marginal part-time employment, fixed-term employment, temporary part-time and full-time employment, and self-employment without employees. [2]The group of persons in standard employment also includes self-employed persons similar trend: like their female counterparts, men increasingly work part time, but they usually work more hours per week, and part-time employment is at a much lower level overall. In 2016, only 7% of men worked part time, compared to 54% who had permanent full-time positions. This means the proportion of men in standard employment is almost twice as high as that of women.

Moreover, it is still mostly women who interrupt their employment for a prolonged period to care for their children. Although more and more German fathers now share in the family work, they only do so selectively, not on an ongoing basis. For instance, many will take their 2 months of so-called paternal leave, but hardly any of them are prepared to reduce their working hours for a longer period of time. This is because men in particular are under the impression that their desire to work part time is interpreted as a decision not to pursue a career. As a consequence, women have a substantially shorter working life than men (Granados and Wrohlich 2018; Brandt 2017; Grunow 2013; Evertsson and Grunow 2012).

There's another aspect to this: women and men work in different occupations. Payment in the so-called female occupations is typically lower than in so-called male occupations, despite the fact that the work performed is comparable (Allmendinger and von den Driesch 2015; Charles and Grusky 2004).

These vast differences in the employment situation of women and men are bound to have an effect on their financial situation. Because German employers still do not pay the same wages for comparable work, and because women tend to work fewer hours, their monthly income is substantially smaller than that of men. Frequently they don't even earn enough to pay for their daily expenses, let alone for a sufficient old-age pension. As a consequence, many retired women strongly depend on pensions derived from their husbands' pension or on government assistance (cf. Allmendinger and von den Driesch 2015; Bettio et al. 2013). Even among the age cohorts retiring until 2015, women's own old-age pensions continued to be lower than the pensions derived from their husbands' earnings, especially in West Germany. Put in slightly exaggerated terms, for West German women, despite their higher average levels of education, the marriage market continued to be more lucrative than the labor market. In 2016, the widow's pensions in West Germany (€610) were slightly lower than pensions based on women's own earnings (€631) for the very first time (DRV 2017).

This is a disastrous situation. Women are expected to earn their own living. Their participation in the workforce is considered a given. This is evident not only in Germany's welfare (Hartz IV) and alimony legislation but also in rising divorce rates, which suggest that women should not rely on pension entitlements derived from their husbands' earnings. Today, one in three marriages ends in divorce (cf. Destatis 2017c). Women are aware of this and strive to be independent. We consistently found in our research women and men who want to be financially independent and build successful careers but do not want to forget having children and friends and relationships in which both partners support each other (Allmendinger 2017; Allmendinger et al. 2013a).

In other words, women in particular are in a predicament. On the one hand, there is a regulatory framework and their individual desire to be financially independent, have children, and live as a couple. On the other hand, the general conditions limit their opportunities and put obstacles in their way. What needs to change?

2 How to Increase Gender Equity in the Labor Market

The only way to improve women's employment rates, working hours, and salary structures is by creating the general conditions to support these ends. This calls for efforts from policy makers and business leaders alike.

We need a binding women's quota to make it easier for highly qualified women to break through the glass ceiling into senior management positions. The share of women in the boardrooms of the top 200 DAX-listed companies is just 8% on average (cf. DIW 2018). Likewise, we have to look at wage levels. If public and private employers in Germany were finally to provide equal pay for comparable work—that is, if starting salaries and salary growth in the so-called female and male occupations were to become more alike—we would likely see more men willing to work in service occupations, for instance as day care teachers or nurses. This would also help raise the social status of these occupations, which, in turn, would presumably lead to higher salaries.

Furthermore, we have to redouble our efforts to make it easier for parents to balance their work and family lives. At first glance, much has already changed in this respect. In Germany, parents are legally entitled to a "parents' allowance" (*Elterngeld*) and day care for their one- and two-year-olds. Day care and preschool services are being expanded, and more and more schools offer all-day activities and support for children and adolescents. Many employers have introduced schemes that have earned them a certification for being family-friendly. For instance, they offer flexible working hours to enable women to re-enter the workforce, albeit with the abovementioned consequences. After returning from parental leave, most women work part time, a status they rarely manage to escape. This means they are denied a real opportunity to make a living for themselves and their children, or build a successful career, based on their own work (cf. Grunow et al. 2011).

If we want to find a way out of this dilemma, we have to start with what causes the differences in male and female employment trajectories. We have to talk about time: about unpaid time, spent with our families and as caregivers, and about paid time, spent at the workplace. We have to reach an agreement about the kind of society that we believe is both worth living in and able to survive.

The European Commission is currently working on guidelines proposing that 70% of women and 85% of men should be in gainful employment. Now add to this the number of people who are no longer capable of work and you end up with a society in which all people work full time (cf. Frazer et al. 2014). But how, then, are they supposed to find the time to raise their children and take care of the elderly? Time for friends, time for recreation, time for continuing education, and for social involvement? Aren't these the kinds of things a community needs, things that define a good life?

This means we have to find better and fairer ways of redistributing paid and unpaid work. Here we see two possibilities: Paid and unpaid work can be distributed more evenly over the life course and more equally between the sexes. As a consequence, people would not only gain valuable extra years that they could use for themselves, their health, family, friends, and society. We can also expect the financial situation of women and men, their earnings and pensions, to become more alike.

3 Redistributing (Working) Hours Over the Life Course

People today not only live longer, they also live longer in better health. For more than 170 years, life expectancy has risen by an average of 3 months per year, or 6 h per day (cf. Fig. 2, based on data from HMD 2018).

The extreme increase in life expectancy is caused by a decline in the risk of death from the age of 80. Even while one generation is still alive, their chances of survival, compared to the previous generation, are increasing. This is mainly the result of improved living conditions, medical progress, and generally a healthier lifestyle (Oeppen and Vaupel 2002). In addition to the higher chances of survival and the increase in life expectancy, we are also seeing the ageing of particularly large birth cohorts in the baby boomer generation. Year after year, the baby boomer cohorts of the 1950s and 1960s are moving upwards in the population pyramid. At the same time, fewer and fewer children are being born. As a result, the German population is shrinking and growing older.

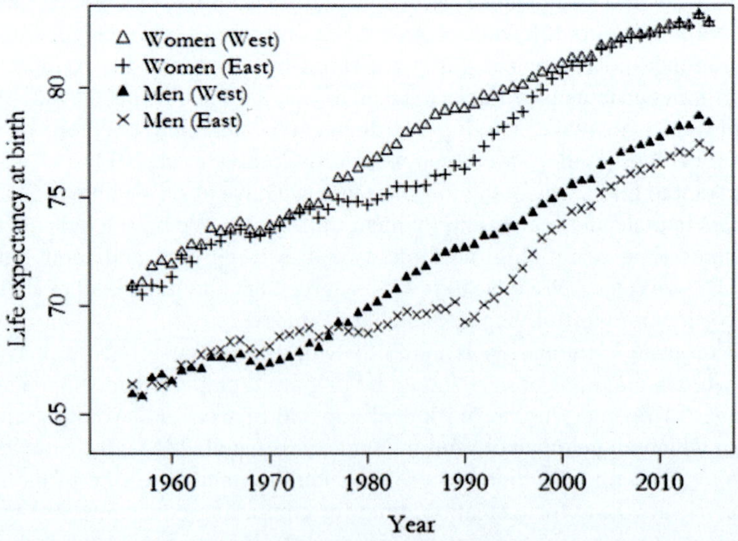

Fig. 2 Life expectancy at birth in Germany, 1954–2015 (cf. Fig. 2, based on data from HMD 2018)

This demographic trend also has effects on the labor market. Even today, there is one pensioner for every three people of working age. And this ratio will shift dramatically in the near future, at the expense of the younger generation. As soon as 2030, we will have fewer than two working-age persons for every pensioner. Furthermore, it is comparatively rare for older persons to still be working. 61% of men and 51% of women in that age bracket are working (Destatis 2017a). Those who are not working have frequently taken advantage of the common practice of early retirement. Others who want to work find it difficult to re-enter the labor market because of their age. Here, society wastes valuable potential and skills.

As people grow older, not only are fewer of them still part of the workforce, they also work shorter hours. Whereas persons under 60 have an average (contractual) workload of 36 h per week (men: 40 h, women: 31 h), persons aged 60 and older work 31 h per week (men: 35 h, women: 26 h). At first glance, the differences seem to be surprisingly small, but this is because we are only looking at the working hours of those who actually work. If we consider the hours worked by all persons within one age group, persons aged 60 and older only work an average of 5 h per week. Persons under 60, by contrast, work an average of 27 h per week (data source: Federal Statistics Office, micro census).

Based on the facts about demographic development and labor market participation, we can conclude the following: If older persons continue to work as little as they do today, the total volume of hours worked in Germany will drop dramatically. In the next 10 years alone, the number of working hours would decrease by approximately 8% (cf. Vaupel and Loichinger 2006). To keep the present number of hours worked at a stable level, the average working hours of 60- to 64-year-olds would have to increase from 16 to 20. Moreover, the 50- to 60-year-olds would have to work as many hours as the 35- to 49-year-olds (i. e., an average of 31 h per week). That is, for social prosperity to remain at its present level, we would have to make older people work more. However, if we also enable persons aged up to 70 years to stay in the workforce to some extent, other age groups would have to shoulder less of the burden. The group of 20- to 40-year-olds, for example, would have more time to juggle the competing tasks of launching their careers and starting a family. Persons in this age bracket could reduce their paid work to put a stronger focus on family and children without suffering disadvantages with respect to their careers. It would become easier to balance work and family responsibilities, and the so-called rush hour of life would be slowed down somewhat.

So instead of expecting people to work longer, we should try to find different ways of distributing working time over the life course. To accomplish this goal, we need to create a supportive regulatory and workplace environment. Legislators have to enable flexible transitions into retirement rather than adhere to rigid age limits. A model that calls on everybody to work longer and longer will not get us anywhere. Rather, older employees should be able to reduce their working hours and receive a partial pension. Working fewer hours can also help reduce physical strain, meaning that people can remain part of the workforce longer than they do now. The foundation for all of this must be a broad-based and solid education and training that can repeatedly serve as the basis for further education and professional development. At the same time, we need a continuing education system that deserves this title, empowering people to stay in the workforce for a long time. Employers can create new incentives to change the age structure of their employees, for instance by introducing more recreational opportunities or physical exercises as part of the daily routine. This would benefit not only the economy but also the people, both young and old.

4 Redistributing (Working) Time Between Women and Men

A few decades ago, it was still quite common for the husband to work 100%, whereas the wife did not work at all. She was in sole charge of the entire household. This model then evolved into a ratio of 100 to 50%, that is, female part-time employment, with women earning a little extra, as it were. If we now move towards a ratio of 100 to 100, meaning that both men and women work full time, there would hardly be any time left for family or caregiving work. But this model is not what women and men want; neither will it enable society to survive.

The unequal division of housework and childcare continues to stand in the way of actual gender equity. In two out of three couples in West Germany, women are in sole charge of housework and childcare (cf. Hobler et al. 2017; Goldstein et al. 2010). One main reason for this is the low level of support from public institutions. Although German parents are now legally entitled to day care for children older than one, there are not yet enough places for every child, especially in the western parts of the country. Having children and a career is still considered almost irreconcilable in Germany. Mothers who want to return to the workplace after taking a child-related break frequently find their salaries and chances of promotion to be lower than those of women with uninterrupted employment histories. This also means they face a higher risk of poverty in old age.

There is another aspect that must not be ignored in this context: caregiving. Even today, almost three million people in Germany are in need of nursing care. Of these, 73% are being cared for at home (Destatis 2017b). And the primary caregivers continue to be wives and daughters (cf. Leopold et al. 2014). For most of them, full-time employment is no longer possible once they start caring for a loved one. That is why improving the situation of women also means improving the situation of nursing care. Children, caregiving, and career must no longer be a matter of either-or in our society.

The classic division of employment and housework has reached its limits. We therefore need to come to a more equal distribution of paid and unpaid work between women and men. If we were to raise women's marginal part-time employment to substantial part-time or marginal full-time employment, and reduce men's working hours accordingly, the total volume of work would not decrease. The only change would be in the way the work is divided between men and women. Women want to work more than marginal part time, preferably 30 to 34 h, to be able to stand on their own feet financially. Likewise, men, especially those in the younger generation, want to work fewer hours. They do not want to work like their fathers, 50 h and more, and hardly get to see their families (Allmendinger 2017).

If the standard working time were reduced to 32 h per week, everybody—not just mothers and fathers—would have the opportunity to work only 4 days a week, for example. This new standard working time must be seen in the context of people's entire working lives. In certain stages of life, it would thus be possible to work more hours, for instance right after finishing one's vocational training or university education, or when the children leave home and the parents are still independent. If the family demands more time, or if we need time for ourselves, these periods of extra work could be used to set off periods of marginal part-time work or employment interruptions. The economy would profit from this new standard working time. Productivity would increase because employers would be able to make much better use of women's excellent education. And it is fair to assume that burn-out caused by highly challenging physical and mental activities would diminish. That would be good for public health, including health in old age.

If we start negotiating new working-time models, we also have to keep in mind that unpaid work, meaning household work, is still predominantly performed by women. In many partnerships, it is them who do the laundry, go shopping, clean the house, or iron the garments (cf. Destatis 2015; Goldstein et al. 2010). It is important to raise both social pressure and social acceptance to encourage men to do their share in this area as well.

Of course, introducing new working-time models presumes that companies support these efforts, for instance by creating part-time management positions, or team-based management arrangements that make it easier to keep the work going in the absence of a colleague. To reach this goal, employers must first bid farewell to the "culture of presence." Efficiency does not come from permanent presence at the workplace. We have already made some progress in that regard. Employers increasingly understand that their employees are not necessarily more productive simply because they are physically present all the time. Now that is not to say that physical presence at the workplace will become completely obsolete, but in cases where it is necessary, it is possible to concentrate such times in a reasonable manner and to schedule meetings in a way so that everybody can attend.

But we also need a family policy that sends clear messages, supporting women and men in their desire to live in partnerships of equals. To foster a more egalitarian distribution of paid and unpaid work in German households, the federal government in 2007 introduced a parental allowance (*Elterngeld*) for fathers, which is tied to taking parental leave. Of the children born in 2007, about one in six fathers took advantage of parental leave; of the children born in 2014, it was more than one in three. However, fathers of children born in 2014 only took an average of just over 3 months of parental leave, whereas mothers took almost a full year (cf. Destatis 2016). A new parental allowance called *Elterngeld plus*, paid since July 2015, is another important step in the right direction. It is designed to support a more equal division of paid and unpaid work. Under this new scheme, if mothers or fathers decide to work part time after the birth of their child, they receive a benefit to compensate for their loss of income. Furthermore, they are entitled to receive the parental allowance for a longer period of time (up to 24 months) and enjoy more flexibility in dividing parental leave time between them.

Of course, parents in part-time employment also need a good and reliable infrastructure for their children. That kind of infrastructure consists of more than financial transfers, which more often than not do not reach the children. Good pre-school institutions and good schools with afternoon programming relieve the parents while providing the children with equal opportunities at an early age.

Behind most of the laws that have promoted gender equality in the past, women in particular have been the driving force. Following the latest Bundestag elections (legislature period 2017 to 2021), however, less than one in three members of the German Bundestag is female.

It is therefore particularly interesting to observe what gender equality policy approaches the new Bundestag—with almost 70% of elected members being male and thus the dominant gender group—and the Federal Government will pursue.

We must use the opportunities brought on by higher life expectancy in good health by redistributing paid and unpaid work more evenly across the life course and between the sexes. In doing so, we will not only gain valuable extra years, in old age and in earlier phases of life. We would also achieve a fairer distribution of work, promoting an equitable co-existence of living spaces. Women and men would be able to lead a whole life, including family, friends, hobbies, continuing education, and volunteer work. It would also be a more just society, because it would provide women and men with similar opportunities. This would mean a big step towards a situation where caregiving and maintaining a career are no longer mutually exclusive.

References

Allmendinger, J. 2017. *Das Land, in dem wir leben wollen. Wie die Deutschen sich ihre Zukunft vorstellen [The kind of country we want to live in. How Germans imagine their future]*. München: Pantheon.

Allmendinger, J., J. Haarbrücker, and F. Fliegner (coop.). 2013a. *Lebensentwürfe heute. Wie junge Frauen und Männer in Deutschland leben wollen. Kommentierte Ergebnisse der Befragung 2012 [Life plans today. How young women and men want to live in Germany. Commented results of the 2012 survey]*. Discussion Paper P 2013–002. Berlin: Wissenschaftszentrum Berlin für Sozialforschung (WZB).

Allmendinger, J., L. Hipp, and S. Stuth. 2013b. *Atypical Employment in Europe 1996-2011*. Discussion Paper P 2013–003. Berlin: Wissenschaftszentrum Berlin für Sozialforschung (WZB).

Allmendinger, J., and E. von den Driesch. 2015. *An ever closer union among the peoples of Europe? Rising Inequalities in the EU and their social, economic and political impacts*. Brussels: European Commission. http://ec.europa.eu/research/social-sciences/pdf/policy_reviews/kina26814enc.pdf. Accessed March 3, 2021.

Bettio, F., P. Tinios, and G. Betti. 2013. *The Gender Gap in Pensions*. Luxembourg: Publications Office of the European Union.

Brandt, G. 2017. Elternzeit von Vätern als Verhandlungssache in Partnerschaften [Fathers' Parental Leave as a Matter of Negotiation in Partnerships]. *Kölner Zeitschrift für Soziologie und Sozialpsychologie* 69 (4): 593–622.

Bundesagentur für Arbeit. 2017. *Die Arbeitsmarktsituation von Frauen und Männern 2016 [The labor market situation of women and men 2016]*. Berichte: Blickpunkt Arbeitsmarkt. Nürnberg.

Charles, M., and D. Grusky. 2004. *Occupational Ghettos: The Worldwide Segregation of Women and Men*. Stanford, CA: Stanford University Press.

Destatis. 2015. *Wie die Zeit vergeht. Ergebnisse zur Zeitverwendung in Deutschland 2012/2013 [How times flies. Results on the use of time in Germany 2012/2013]*. Wiesbaden: Statistisches Bundesamt.

Destatis. 2016. *Elterngeld für Geburten 2014 nach Kreisen [Parental allowance for 2014 births by district]*. Wiesbaden: Statistisches Bundesamt.

Destatis. 2017a. *Arbeitsmarkt. Statistisches Jahrbuch 2017 [Labor market. Statistical Yearbook 2017]*. Wiesbaden: Statistisches Bundesamt.

Destatis. 2017b. *Bevölkerung und Erwerbstätigkeit. Statistik der rechtskräftigen Beschlüsse in Eheauflösungssachen (Scheidungsstatistik) und Statistik der Aufhebung von Lebenspartnerschaften [Population and employment. Statistics on legally valid decisions in cases of dissolution of marriage (divorce statistics) and statistics on dissolution of civil partnerships]*. Fachserie 1: 1.4–2015. Wiesbaden: Statistisches Bundesamt.

Destatis. 2017c. *Pflegestatistik 2015. Pflege im Rahmen der Pflegeversicherung. Deutschlandergebnisse [Care statistics 2015. Care within the framework of care insurance. German results]*. Wiesbaden: Statistisches Bundesamt.

DRV – Deutsche Rentenversicherung Bund. 2017. *Rentenversicherung in Zahlen 2017 [German statutory pension insurance in figures 2017]*. Berlin.

DIW – Deutsches Institut für Wirtschaftsforschung. 2018. *Managerinnen-Barometer 2018 [Female manager barometer 2018]*. DIW Wochenbericht 1 + 2. Berlin.

Evertsson, M., and D. Grunow. 2012. Women's work interruptions and career prospects in Germany and Sweden. *International Journal of Sociology and Social Policy* 32 (9): 561–575.

Frazer, H., A. C. Guio, E. Marlier, B. Vanhercke, and T. Ward. 2014. *Putting the fight against poverty and social exclusion at the heart of the EU agenda: a contribution to the Mid-Term Review of the Europe 2020 Strategy*. Research Paper 15. Brussels: European Social Observatory.

Goldstein, J. R., M. R. Kreyenfeld, J. Huinink, D. Konietzka, and H. Trappe. 2010. *Familie und Partnerschaft in Ost- und Westdeutschland: Ergebnisse im Rahmen des Projektes "Demographic differences in life course dynamics in Eastern and Western Germany" [Family and partnership in East and West Germany: Results of the project "Demographic differences in life course dynamics in Eastern and Western Germany"]*. Rostock: Max-Planck-Institut für demografische Forschung.

Granados, P., and K. Wrohlich. 2018. Gender Pay Gap besonders groß bei niedrigen und hohen Löhnen [Gender pay gap particularly large for low and high wages]. *DIW Wochenbericht* 10: 173–179.

Grunow, D. 2013. Zwei Schritte vor, eineinhalb Schritte zurück. Geschlechtsspezifische Arbeitsteilung und Sozialisation aus Perspektive des Lebensverlaufs [Two steps forward, one and a half steps back. Gender-based Division of Labour and Socialisation as a Matter of Biography]. *Zeitschrift für Soziologie der Erziehung und Sozialisation* 4: 384–398.

Grunow, D., S. Aisenbrey, and M. Evertsson. 2011. Familienpolitik, Bildung und Berufskarrieren von Müttern in Deutschland, USA und Schweden [Motherhood, family policy, education, and careers in Germany, the US, and Sweden]. *Kölner Zeitschrift für Soziologie und Sozialpsychologie* 63 (3): 395–430.

Hobler, D., C. Klenner, S. Pfahl, P. Sopp, and A. Wagner. 2017. Wer leistet unbezahlte Arbeit. Hausarbeit, Kindererziehung und Pflege im Geschlechtervergleich. Aktuelle Auswertungen aus dem WSI GenderDatenPortal [Who performs unpaid work. Housekeeping, child-rearing and care in a gender comparison. Current evaluations from the WSI GenderDatenPortal]. *WSI Report* 35. Düsseldorf: Wirtschafts- und Sozialwissenschaftliches Institut (WSI).

HMD. 2018. The Human Mortality Database. University of California, Berkeley (USA), and Max Planck Institute for Demographic Research (Germany). www.humanmortality.de. Accessed March 3, 2021.

Leopold, T., M. Raab, and H. Engelhardt. 2014. The Transition to Parent Care: Costs, Commitments and Caregiver Selection Among Children. *Journal of Marriage and Family* 76 (2): 300–318.

Oeppen, J., and J. Vaupel. 2002. Broken Limits to Life Expectancy. *Science* 296: 1029–1031.

Stuth, S. et al. 2018. Prekarität in Deutschland?! DZA Discussion Paper. Berlin.

Vaupel, J., and E. Loichinger. 2006. Redistributing Work in Aging Europe. *Science* 312 (5782): 1911–1913.

Health Literacy in Europe: The Concept, Its Impact and Application

Kristine Sørensen

1 Introduction

Health literacy—the ability to understand and use health information—depends on individual skills and also on the complexity of the health information being presented. Most clinicians assume patients understand everything but this is frequently not the case. Patients may not realize they don't quite understand, or even when they know they don't understand, they are afraid or ashamed to tell the clinician. People with lower health literacy, for example, might not know how to take their medications or why they have to follow specific doctor's instructions (Nielsen-Bohlman et al. 2004). Patients with low or limited health literacy have poor outcomes from a number of disease processes which results in increased costs to society. In 2003, a government study in the United States of America found that 89 million Americans had limited health literacy skills and they came from all segments of society (Eichler et al. 2009). The emerging field of health literacy in the US stimulated also a growing interest from various stakeholders involved in European policy, research and practice. On the European political agenda, health literacy was associated with patient empowerment in the health strategy *Together for Health 2008-2013* of the *European Union* (European Commission 2007) and later integrated into the *Health 2020* strategy of the European Office of the *World Health Association* (World Health Organization's European Office 2011). With regard to research, health literacy came into focus due to previous research conducted in North America, which revealed that low health literacy had considerable impact on people's health outcome and the quality of healthcare services (Berkman et al. 2010). For a start, the European research focused primarily on patients' health literacy

K. Sørensen (✉)
Global Health Literacy Academy, Risskov, Denmark
e-mail: contact@globalhealthliteracyacademy.org

B. Schmitz-Luhn, C. Woopen (eds.), *Justice over the Course of Life*, Schriften zu Gesundheit und Gesellschaft - Studies on Health and Society 1,
https://doi.org/10.1007/978-3-030-86449-1_9

(Twickler et al. 2009). Later, EU-funded research entailed a broader public health perspective including funding of a population study in eight countries (Sørensen et al. 2015), health literacy among the elderly (Geboers et al. 2015) and health literacy and chronic diseases exemplified by the study of Diabetes literacy (Van den Broucke et al. 2014). Integrating health literacy into practice for improving health has been carried out by healthcare providers, the educational sector and schools and in the broader community (Kickbusch et al. 2013).

2 The Concept of Health Literacy

The concept of health literacy was mentioned in an American social policy paper for the first time in 1974 (Simonds 1974). However, it got increased attention from the medical field in the mid-1990s, when studies showed that patients with low health literacy were faced with various disparities in the United States (Rudd et al. 1999). Meanwhile, health literacy was presented in the *Glossary of Health Promotion* by the *European Office* of the *World Health Organization* in Copenhagen as rooted in educational theory (Nutbeam 1998). Interestingly, the European health literacy discourse is influenced by three major streams of thought which are still traceable in some of the most commonly applied definitions as illustrated in Fig. 1 (Sørensen 2014). The first stream concerns patient empowerment and quality of care represented by the definition of the *Institute of Medicine* of the United States which defines health literacy as the individuals' capacity to obtain, process and understand basic health information and services needed to make appropriate health decisions (Nielsen-Bohlman et al. 2004). The second stream originates from the field of literacy and education exemplified by Nutbeam who defined health literacy as the personal, cognitive and social skills which determine the ability of individuals to gain access to, understand, and use information to promote and maintain good health (Nutbeam 1998). The third stream is associated with citizens' empowerment and

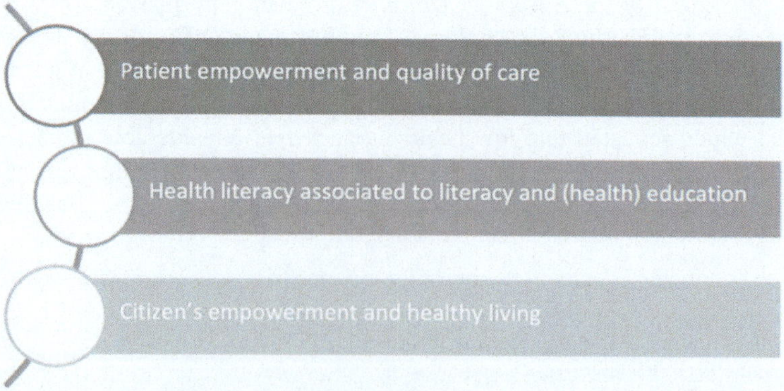

Fig. 1 The European health literacy discourse is influenced by three streams of thought (Sørensen 2014)

healthy living represented by Kickbusch and Maag who provide a much broader definition stating that health literacy concerns the ability to make sound health decisions in the context of everyday life—at home, in the community, at the workplace, the healthcare system, the market place and the political arena (Kickbusch et al. 2005).

Yet, it becomes clear when studying health literacy definitions in more detail that they overlap more than they differ. The systematic review from 2012 conducted by the *European Health Literacy Consortium* identified a list of essential components from 17 definitions and integrated them into a comprehensive definition. It suggests that health literacy is linked to literacy and entails people's knowledge, motivation and competencies to access, understand, appraise and apply information to form judgment and take decisions in everyday life in terms of healthcare, disease prevention and health promotion to maintain and improve quality of life during the life course (Sørensen et al. 2012). This definition was accompanied by a conceptual model reflecting the integrative definition and highlighting how health literacy is influenced by personal determinants, situational determinants and societal determinants. In turn, health literacy influences health service use and costs, health behavior and health status, participation and empowerment, as well as sustainability and equity (Sørensen et al. 2012).

3 Measuring Health Literacy in Europe

The definition and conceptual model served as basis for the development of the *European Health Literacy Questionnaire*, called the *HLS-EU-Q* (Sørensen et al. 2013). It was the first tool to measure health literacy in populations. Previous tools focused primarily on patients' (health) literacy such as the *Rapid Estimate of Adult Literacy in Medicine (REALM)* (Parker et al. 1995), the *Test of Functional Health Literacy in Adults (TOEFHLA)* (Baker et al. 1999) and the *Newest Vital Sign (NVS)* (Weiss et al. 2005). While inventories were made on health literacy measurements to keep up with the developments (Haun et al. 2012, 2014), a database is now available from *Boston University* called the *Health Literacy Tool Shed* [https://healthliteracy.bu.edu/] which includes almost 200 tools. Health literacy is content and context specific, which is illustrated very well by the variety of tools available. Some of the key differences include their specific health literacy focus (e.g. information seeking, critical thinking, literacy and numeracy), the way they are administered, their design and number of items and how they are scored and correlate with other health literacy tests, as well as their general target audience (World Health Organization 2013).

The *European Health Literacy Survey* was conducted in Austria, Bulgaria, Germany, Greece, Ireland, the Netherlands, Poland and Spain. It revealed that almost one in two face difficulties in managing health while accessing, understanding, appraising and applying information to form judgement and make decisions. For people with low education, low economic status, for the elderly and migrants there was an even higher risk indicating a strong social gradient for health literacy and its impact on health. Essentially, the survey showed that limited health literacy is a neglected public health challenge in Europe (Sørensen et al. 2015).

4 The Impact of Health Literacy in Practice

Studying the impact of health literacy in practice it becomes clear that it is not always the patients who are to be blamed. Governance systems are not only short on offering protections and enhancing capabilities; in some cases, they are producing new vulnerabilities (United Nations Development Programme 2014). Parker introduced a dual responsibility related to health literacy to bridge the gap. Firstly, one can educate people to more resourcefulness and by doing so advance their health literacy and, secondly, one can make the task/role/situation/context they have to cope with less demanding and, hence, reduce the complexity (Parker and Ratzan 2010). She implied that health literacy was about people and patients' competency to match the complexity of systems. However, in order to provide a real change for future health that will benefit patients and citizens in a more profound and sustainable manner it may be necessary to rephrase the dual responsibility when redesigning care that supports patient empowerment towards the health systems, thus strengthening their competency to match the systems' complexity.

Health literacy is a concept which fosters access to health and puts citizens and patients at the center of health and healthcare. In support of redesigning healthcare systems to become more health literacy friendly, the *Institute of Medicine* recommended ten attributes to be developed by health organizations. The ten attributes include: Leadership; Planning, Evaluation and Improvements; Preparation of Workforce; Consumer Involvement; Meeting the Needs of all; Effective Communication; Easy Access; Design of Easy to Use Materials; Targeting High Risk Groups; and Explanation of Coverage and Costs (Brach et al. 2012).

It is imperative to accelerate health literacy on the European agenda to strengthen the citizens' role with regard to their health, to improve health outcomes and to reduce the growing burden on healthcare systems (Quaglio et al. 2017). The *European Commission*, for instance, highlighted health literacy in the *Beating Cancer Plan* (European Commission 2021). Furthermore, at national levels European countries are increasingly implementing health literacy policies and strategies to bridge the inequality gap (Welsh Assembly Government 2011), ensure better quality of services (NHS Scotland 2017) and increasing health literacy of populations (Schaeffer et al. 2018).

5 Conclusion

The European Health Literacy Project served as an important eye-opener and a call for action to bridge the gap of limited health literacy in Europe. The growing evidence can be used as a catalyst for change and social justice. The recommendations include

- **Dare to compare**—measure, benchmark, evaluate, learn, change accordingly—stop, start, continue initiatives and integrate with existing structures.
- **Make healthy choices easy choices to make**—involve health professionals as choice architects.
- **Involve patients and citizens**—they know the enabling and hindering factors for good care and improvement of their own health.
- **Redesign health infrastructure**—modernization of the healthcare system towards full partnerships with patients and consumers and use of new technologies.
- **Investment in health literacy organizational activities**—aiming at better health and safety at work, health promotion and disease prevention, lifelong learning to improve adaptability of workforce, training and education of health professionals.

By building the health literacy capacity of people, communities, organizations and systems it is possible to create a health literate society where no one is left behind.

References

Baker, D. W., M. Williams, R. Parker, J. A. Gazmararian, and J. Nurss. 1999. Development of a brief test to measure functional health literacy. *Patient Education and Counseling* 38 (1): 33–42. http://www.ncbi.nlm.nih.gov/pubmed/14528569. Accessed June 30, 2021.

Berkman, N. D., T. C. Davis, and L. McCormack. 2010. Health literacy: what is it? *Journal of Health Communication* 15 (2): 9–19. http://www.ncbi.nlm.nih.gov/pubmed/20845189. Accessed April 12, 2021.

Brach, C., D. Keller, L. M. Hernandez, C. Baur, R. Parker, B. Dreyer, P. Schyve, A. J. Lemerise, and D. Schillinger. 2012. *Ten Attributes of Health Literate Health Care Organizations*. Discussion Paper. Washington, DC: National Academy of Medicine.

Eichler, K., S. Wieser, and U. Brügger. 2009. The costs of limited health literacy: a systematic review. *International Journal of Public Health*. 54 (5): 313–324. http://www.ncbi.nlm.nih.gov/pubmed/19644651. Accessed April 12, 2021.

European Commission. 2007. *Together for Health: A Strategic Approach for the EU 2008-2013*. Brussels. Available from: http://ec.europa.eu/health/ph_overview/Documents/strategy_wp_en.pdf. Accessed April 12, 2021

European Commission. 2021. Europe's Beating Cancer Plan. Available from: https://ec.europa.eu/info/strategy/priorities-2019-2024/promoting-our-european-way-life/european-health-union/cancer-plan-europe_en. Accessed June 30, 2021.

Geboers, B., J. S. Brainard, Y. K. Loke, C. J. M. Jansen, C. Salter, S. A. Reijneveld, and A. F. de Winter. 2015. The association of health literacy with adherence in older adults, and its role in interventions: a systematic meta-review. *BMC Public Health* 15: Article no. 903. http://www.ncbi.nlm.nih.gov/pubmed/26377316. Accessed April 12, 2021.

Haun, J., S. Luther, V. Dodd, and P. Donaldson. 2012. Measurement variation across health literacy assessments: implications for assessment selection in research and practice. *Journal of Health Communication* 17 Supplement 3: 141–159. http://www.ncbi.nlm.nih.gov/pubmed/23030567. Accessed June 30, 2021.

Haun, J. N., M. A. Valerio, L. A. McCormack, K. Sørensen, and M. K. Paasche-Orlow. 2014. Health Literacy Measurement: An Inventory and Descriptive Summary of 51 Instruments. *Journal of Health Communication* 19 Supplement 2: 302–333. http://www.tandfonline.com/doi/abs/10.1080/10810730.2014.936571. Accessed April 12, 2021.

Kickbusch, I., S. Wait, and D. Maag. 2005. Navigating health. The role of health literacy. Alliance for Health and the Future. International Longevity Centre-UK. https://ilcuk.org.uk/navigating-health-the-role-of-health-literacy/. Accessed April 12, 2021.

Kickbusch, I., J. Pelikan, F. Apfel, and T. Agis. 2013. *Health literacy: the solid facts*. 1st ed. Copenhagen: World Health Organization Regional Office for Europe.

NHS Scotland. 2017. Making it easier: a health literacy action plan 2017-2025. Available from: https://www.gov.scot/publications/making-easier-health-literacy-action-plan-scotland-2017-2025/. Accessed March 22, 2021.

Nielsen-Bohlman, L. T., A. M. Panzer, and D. A. Kindig. 2004. *Health Literacy: A Prescription to End Confusion*. San Francisco: The National Academies Press.

Nutbeam, D. 1998. Health Promotion Glossary. *Health Promotion International* 13 (4): 349–364. https://academic.oup.com/heapro/article/13/4/349/563193. Accessed June 30, 2021.

Parker, R. M., D. W. Baker, M. Williams, and J. Nurss. 1995. The test of functional health literacy in adults. A new instrument for measuring patients' literacy skills. *Journal of General Internal Medicine* 10 (10): 537–541. https://link.springer.com/article/10.1007/BF02640361. Accessed April 12, 2021.

Parker, R. M., and S. C. Ratzan. 2010. Health literacy: a second decade of distinction for Americans. *Journal of Health Communication* 15 Supplement 2: 20–33. http://www.ncbi.nlm.nih.gov/pubmed/20845190. Accessed April 12, 2021.

Quaglio, G., K. Sørensen, P. Rübig, L. Bertinato, H. Brand, T. Karapiperis, I. Dinca, T. Peetso, K. Kadenbach, C. Dario. 2017. Accelerating the health literacy agenda in Europe. *Health Promotion International* 32 (6): 1074-1080. https://academic.oup.com/heapro/article/32/6/1074/2951033. Accessed April 12, 2021

Rudd, R. R., B. Moeykens, and T. Colton. 1999. Health and Literacy: A review of the medical and public health literature. In *Annual Review of Adult Learning and Literacy*. Vol. 1, chapter 5, eds. J. P. Comings, C. Smith, and B. Garner. San Francisco, CA: Jossey-Bass.

Schaeffer, D., K. Hurrelmann, U. Bauer, and K. Kolpatzik (eds.): National Action Plan. Health Literacy. Promoting Health Literacy in Germany. Berlin: KomPart 2018. Available from: https://www.nap-gesundheitskompetenz.de/. Accessed March 22, 2021.

Simonds, S. K. 1974. Health education as social policy. *Health Education Monographs* 2: 1–25.

Sørensen, K. 2014. Health literacy in Europe: the concept, its impact and application using the example of diabetes literacy. **ceres**; Workshop: Health literacy, Patient Orientation, and Justice, Universität zu Köln, Germany, September 5, 2014.

Sørensen, K., S. Van den Broucke, J. Fullam, G. Doyle, J. Pelikan, Z. Slonska, H. Brand, and Consortium Health Literacy Project European (HLS-EU). 2012. Health literacy and public health: a systematic review and integration of definitions and models. *BMC Public Health* 12 (1): 80. http://www.biomedcentral.com/1471-2458/12/80. Accessed April 12, 2021.

Sørensen K., S. Van den Broucke, J. Pelikan, J. Fullam, G. Doyle, Z. Slonska, B. Kondilis, V. Stoffels, R. H. Osborne, H. Brand, and Consortium Health Literacy Project European (HLS-EU). 2013. Measuring health literacy in populations: illuminating the design and development process of the European Health Literacy Survey Questionnaire (HLS-EU-Q). *BMC Public Health* 13: Article no. 948. http://www.biomedcentral.com/1471-2458/13/948. Accessed April 12, 2021.

Sørensen, K., J. M. Pelikan, F. Röthlin, K. Ganahl, Z. Slonska, G. Doyle, J. Fullam, B. Kondilis, D. Agrafiotis, E. Uiters, M. Falcon, M. Mensing, K. Tchamov, S. van den Broucke, H. Brand, and HLS-EU Consortium. 2015. Health literacy in Europe: comparative results of the European health literacy survey (HLS-EU). *European Journal of Public Health* 25 (6): 1053–1058. http://www.ncbi.nlm.nih.gov/pubmed/25843827. Accessed June 30, 2021.

Twickler, T. B. M., E. Hoogstraaten, A. Q. Reuwer, L. Singels, K. Stronks, and M.-L. Essink-Bot. 2009. Low literacy and limited health literacy require health care measures. *Nederlands Tijdschrift voor Geneeskunde* 153: A250. http://www.ncbi.nlm.nih.gov/pubmed/19785884. Accessed April 12, 2021.

United Nations Development Programme. 2014. *Human Development Report 2014. Sustaining Human Progress: Reducing Vulnerabilities and Building Resilience.* New York. http://hdr.undp.org/sites/default/files/hdr14-report-en-1.pdf. Accessed April 12, 2021.

Van den Broucke, S., G. Van der Zanden, P. Chang, G. Doyle, D. Levin, J. Pelikan, D. Schillinger, P. Schwarz, K. Sørensen, L. Yardley, and H. Riemenschneider. 2014. Enhancing the effectiveness of diabetes self-management education: the diabetes literacy project. *Hormone and Metabolic Research* 46 (13): 933–938. http://www.ncbi.nlm.nih.gov/pubmed/25337960. Accessed April 12, 2021.

Weiss, B. D., M. Z. Mays, W. Martz, K. M. Castro, D. A. DeWalt, M. P. Pignone, J. Mockbee, and F. A. Hale. 2005. Quick Assessment of Literacy in Primary Care: The Newest Vital Sign. *Annals of Family Medicine* 3 (6): 514–522. https://www.ncbi.nlm.nih.gov/pmc/articles/PMC1466931/. Accessed April 12, 2021.

Welsh Assembly Government. 2011. Fairer Health Outcomes For All. Reducing Inequities in health Strategic Action Plan. Our Healthy Future – Technical Working Paper 2. Cardiff. http://www.wales.nhs.uk/sitesplus/documents/866/5.1%20Appendix%20Fairer%20Outcomes%20for%20All%2DWelsh%20Assembly%20Government%20Document.pdf. Accessed April 12, 2021.

World Health Organization. 2013. *Health Literacy. The solid facts.* Copenhagen.

World Health Organization's European Office. 2011. *The new European policy for health – Health 2020: Vision, values, main directions and approaches.* Baku, Azerbaijan.

Patient Involvement in Health Care: Conceptualisation, Measurement, Uptake and Future Improvement

Oliver Gröne

1 Introduction

The topic of patient involvement (PI) is gaining increasing importance in health services research, health policy and service delivery (Mockford et al. 2012). In the US, *the Patient-Centered Outcomes Research* Institute (PCORI) was established three years ago specifically to bolster research focusing more on patients' needs. *PCORI* funded research requires patients and other stakeholders to be involved in all phases of the study (Selby and Lipstein 2014). In the UK, the *National Institute for Health Research (NIHR)* funded research is not as prescriptive but does require applicants to describe in detail how patients are involved in different stages of research and implementation, a recommendation shared by the *American Hospital Association* (American Hospital Association 2005). At EU level, the *Council of the European Union* emphasizes the need for health care to become more patient centred and strengthen the involvement, in particular, of chronically ill patients (Council of the European Commission 2010). The *Collaborations for Leadership in Applied Health Research*, a newly established partnership of academic institutions and health services providers in the UK that aim at identifying new ways of service provision and bringing new evidence faster into practice, too, emphasize the importance of PI (Renedo et al. 2014).

Patient and public involvement is referred to in many ways, both conceptually and in terms of terminology. Patient involvement is referred to under different terms in the literature, including "patient involvement", "user involvement", "lay involvement" or "patient representation" (Crawford et al. 2002). We will focus here on the term patient involvement (PI), referring both to the involvement of patients in their

O. Gröne (✉)
OptiMedis AG, Hamburg, Germany
e-mail: o.groene@optimedis.de

B. Schmitz-Luhn, C. Woopen (eds.), *Justice over the Course of Life*, Schriften zu Gesundheit und Gesellschaft - Studies on Health and Society 1,
https://doi.org/10.1007/978-3-030-86449-1_10

own care, and the involvement of patients in activities not directly related to their own care, such as representing patient views on activities related to planning, designing, or assessing quality management in hospitals (Groene et al. 2009).

There is growing recognition that PI can make an important contribution to quality improvement, in particular since the definition of what constitutes quality in health care has changed over the last decade. It is now widely accepted that quality is more than good clinical care, but rather reflects a multi-dimensional construct including dimensions such as clinical effectiveness, safety and patient-centredness (Institute of Medicine 2001). These three dimensions of health care quality are now embedded in quality legislation and regulation in many countries (i.e. in the NHS constitution (Department of Health 2008)). Consequently, whereas previously PI was not high on the agenda in most countries—as patients are less likely to get involved or able to contribute to technical discussions of what constitutes clinical effectiveness—it is now widely accepted and anticipated that patients and their representations make substantial contributions to the non-clinical aspects of care (Gerteis et al. 1993). The patient safety literature has shown that patients can also contribute significantly to identifying care factors that potentially lead to harm, or, if harm has occurred already, help learning from an incident in order to avoid it in the future (World Health Organization 2011).

Against this background, the aims of this paper are to review the conceptual basis for the contribution of PI to quality in health care, discuss how best to measure patient involvement, present empirical data on the extent to which patients are currently involved by hospitals in design and learning, and finally offer some reflections on how patient involvement can be improved in the future.

2 Conceptualising Patient Involvement in Health Care: A Means to an End or an End in Itself?

Patient involvement is often seen as a means to an end, in particular as a means to realizing patient-centred care. Patient-centred care is defined as "*health care that establishes a partnership among practitioners, patients, and their families (when appropriate) to ensure that decisions respect patients' wants, needs, and the preferences and that patients have the education and support they need to make decisions and participate in their own care*" (Institute of Medicine 2001). This is increasingly being acknowledged as an integral part of evaluating health care. The origins of patient-centredness in health care can be traced back to the Hippocratic oath, however, it was not until the 1950s that the concept of patient-centred care gained importance in medicine and health services research. At that time the excessive focus of medical care on disease processes as compared to illness experience raised a lot of concerns and Engel and Balint opposed the predominant biomedical model (Balint 1969; Engel 1977). Since then, the focus on patient-centredness has continuously evolved in the literature and in recent years has been greatly emphasized in policy initiatives (Lewin et al. 2001). Yet, patient involvement strategies go beyond involving patients in their own care, and they go beyond making care patient-centred.

Patient involvement is not just a means, but a means, a right in itself (Berwick 2009). It embraces arguments of democratisation (according to which a paternalistic relationship between patient and professional would contradict the notions of democratic societies), operationalised in hospital settings in terms of policies to ensure confidentiality, informed consent, information about treatment and care, and issues related to professional-patient interaction (Roter and Larson 2002; Gerteis et al. 1993). It is not a question whether such issues always lead to better empowerment, participation in health care or even contribute to outcomes—there are ends in themselves. However, frequently, these ends are not met. For example, Schoen and colleagues assessed the experiences of patients with health problems and found that a considerable proportion of patients reported problems with lack of respect for patients' preferences and involvement of family and friends, and more than a third of patients assert that risks of treatments or procedures were not or were only partly explained (Schoen et al. 2005). Similar results were found by Coulter and Jenkinson in a cross-European study of patients' views on the responsiveness of health systems and health care providers (Coulter and Jenkinson 2005). Since patients' rights have become an integral part of definitions of quality of care, quality improvement efforts should strengthen these rights.

Patient involvement is also a means to greater effects. It has implications for patient behaviour, recovery and outcomes. The evidence base concerning health gain and outcomes spans from sociology, over psychology, to medicine, nursing and rehabilitation sciences. Research suggests that patient-involvement is associated with better compliance, patient satisfaction, better recovery and health outcomes, augmentation of tolerance for stress and pain levels, reduced readmission rates and better seeking of follow up care (Hibbard et al. 2005; Balik et al. 2011; Lazarus 2000). In a review of systematic reviews interventions to improve health literacy, interventions to improve clinical decision-making and interventions to improve self-management of chronic diseases, Coulter and Ellins report that a majority of reviews yielded positive effects in terms of improving knowledge, better experience of care, decreased use of resources and improved health behaviour and health status (Coulter and Ellins 2007).

Another rationale for patient-involvement is less prominent in the health care literature, alas; it is an important focus from a quality improvement perspective. In short, in order for organisations to learn, personal context specific knowledge needs to be transferred into codified systematic and formal knowledge. Knowledge-dependent organisations constantly revise knowledge at all organisational levels in order to inform process alignment, innovation, product development and service provision (Nonaka and Takeuchi 1995). In hospitals, the patients' knowledge has traditionally been ignored as a "production factor", ignoring the potential contributions to assessing, improving and implementing work processes. Patients can contribute significantly to health care improvements, in particular through their assessment of non-clinical aspects of care, their assessment of the care environment and their observations and experience with the care process (American Hospital Association 2005; Lorig et al. 2008; Pfaff 2004). However, this information is not always gathered systematically, thus hospitals are missing relevant information for improvement projects. For example, while many hospitals carry out patient surveys, little is known to what extent professionals are aware of the results of patient surveys in their ward, or whether this information is used at all for quality improvement work (Boyer et al. 2006; Davies and Cleary 2005). There are a number of reasons why patient survey data is not systematically used in quality improvement efforts, such as organisational barriers (lack of priority or supporting infrastructures), professional barriers (scepticism, resistance to change) or data related barriers (lack of timely feedback or lack of specificity and discrimination). Quality improvement efforts need to overcome these barriers in order to being able to elicit patients' contributions in processes of organisational learning.

3 Measuring What Is Important to Patients

A key to quality improvement in health care is measurement: without measurement, neither baseline status nor improvements over time are known. Consequently, quality improvement should involve patients to make sure that constructs relevant to patients are captured. Measurement should address both patient assessments of their own care as well as assessments of relevant organisational characteristics.

3.1 Involving Patients in Deciding What Is Being Measured

The involvement of patients and the public has become indispensable in some areas of health services research. This includes for example the process of measure development, be it for measures of patient reported outcomes, satisfaction, experience or other measures where patients' views on their own health or on aspects of care are sought. Evidence (and common wisdom) suggests that conducting focus groups or individual interviews with patients as a starting point for measure development leads to a better understanding of illness experience, domain clarification and to item generation (Streiner and Norman 2003). Likewise, once a measure has been drafted, cognitive interviews are typically conducted with patients in order to assess item comprehension, recall, processing and verbalisation of a response. This type of involvement is not particularly resource intensive and the benefits usually outweigh resource requirements. Patient and public involvement is also increasingly established in other areas of health services research where patients' inputs can help to understand the context of implementing measurement tools, clinical practice guidelines (Boivin et al. 2010) or quality improvement and patient safety interventions (World Health Organization 2011). Patients may not be full collaborators but rather information providers, and the decisions how to interpret and act upon the contributions of patients are still with the researcher. This type of collaboration is not trivial and may cover the whole research process from identifying relevant research issues to refining how these can be assessed in a reliable and valid manner. This contribution should not be underestimated.

In other areas of research, patient and public involvement is highly desirable even if the evidence base or immediate benefits are perhaps less tangible. This includes for example the ongoing collaboration of patients and their representatives in working groups that develop or test outcome measures which could help to challenge tacit or implicit models that underpin measure development. The experience in this field is perhaps more limited, partly because of the lack of good quality evaluations and partly due to the complex intervention that patient and public involvement entails. The success of patient and public involvement in this regard may depend largely on being able to recruit participants with the right experience, cognitive and verbal skills (Conway 2008). If the purpose is to involve representatives of patients and the public, a key question is also how representative these might be? Often, representatives may not reflect the range of patient groups that will ultimately use the measure. In fact, not everybody wants to be involved and in general, less educated patients tend to prefer less involvement than better educated patients (Levinson et al. 2005). Patient involvement strategies, if not carefully designed and conducted may undermine their very purpose by representing the interests and concerns of a limited group of patients only. The involvement of patients and the public in this sense thus needs further examination in terms of the type of patients performing the functions, the criteria used for their selection, the training they receive, the contributions they make to measure development and the consequences of their contributions to care design (Institute for Patient and Family Centred Care 2009). These effects then require careful consideration against resource requirements of patient and public involvement.

Patient and public involvement is probably most challenging when it comes to the most complex tasks, such as interpretation of data on health care quality to guide services design and informed choice decisions. The involvement of patients and the public in contributing to or discussing analysis of data on health care quality is challenging for a variety of reasons. Many of these aspects are highly technical and rely on concepts and language, involve interpretation of statistical concepts, and thus need appropriate explanation. Yet research suggests that patients, even after extensive training, have problems interpreting tables and graphs (Hildon et al. 2012) and taking informed decisions regarding their care based on that information (Peters et al. 2007). Many patients in fact lack the skills, education, knowledge, and motivation to process and constructively assess complex information. The effects of illiteracy and ill-numeracy have appropriately been called a silent epidemic and have major implications throughout the health system (Marcus 2006; Lipkus et al. 2001; Sunstein and Thaler 2003).

The involvement of patients and the public in designing, implementing and interpreting patient-reported outcomes is an exciting field with many developments over the last 5 to 10 years. In some areas, such as measurement design, patient and public involvement has become a common theme, based on the evidence of benefit and little resource requirements. In others, promising experiences emerge, but they require further careful evaluation to make sure that resources are used appropriately.

3.2 Measuring Patient Views of Their Own Care

Patient views regarding the care they receive are usually assessed using standardised questionnaires, even though qualitative research such as in-depth interviews and focus groups are also used to explore patient views. A major limitation to assess and improve patient views is the lack of a gold standard measure (Lewin et al. 2001). This is partly due to the conceptually broad nature of the construct, including a wide range of different constructs, disease-specific and generic measures, different forms of conceptualisation and psychometrics (experience measures, satisfaction measures and gap-based measures), and differences in intent and administration (pre-admission to assess patients' preferences and post-discharge to assess patients views of hospital services) (van Campen et al. 1995). The advantage of generic measures is their global assessment across various dimensions of patient-centredness, while specific measures provide a more in-depth assessment of one or more dimensions. Measures of patient satisfaction or experience are typically administered at discharge or post-discharge. However, depending on the information required to improve the quality of care, measures may require administration before a contact with the health care provider. For example, considering patients' characteristics as an input into the hospital work processes, it may be necessary to elicit preferences for shared decision-making or to understand patients' ability to comprehend and process the information that is exchanged between professionals and patients. While some generic measures of patient-centredness include questions regarding professional's oral expression and listening skills, the actual level of health literacy of the patient and preferences for involvement and decision-making are not routinely assessed. However, without such prior information, information and education strategies employed in hospital settings may have a limited effect. Considering the differences in approaches, administration, timing and conceptual basis, the use of measures to assess patient views should be driven by the information required to improve practice and by the extent to which they support management in improving patient centredness. A single standard measure may not fit all these purposes (Table 1).

3.3 Measuring Organisations' Preparedness for Patient Involvement

In addition to assessing patient views of hospital services, organisational assessment tools allow to assess the underlying characteristics that form patient views. These

Table 1 Selected patient-level measures of patient views care by type

Type of measure	Example
Assessing preferences for decision making role	– Control preferences scale – Decision involvement questionnaire – Problem-solving decision-making scale – Role and information preferences – Focus of authority scale – Information styles questionnaire
Evaluating patient involvement in decision-making	– Observing patient involvement in decision-making scale – Decision support analysis tool – Elements of informed decision-making – Rochester participatory decision-making scale
Assessing patients' perception of involvement	– Satisfaction with decision-making process – Participatory decision-making style – Patients perceived involvement in care scale
Assessing preparation for chronic disease self-management	– Patient activation measure – Health Care Transition measure
Generic measures to assess patient experience	– Hospital Consumer Assessment of Healthcare Providers and Systems – PICKER Survey
Generic measures to assess patient satisfaction	– Press Ganey Associates – Ware's patient satisfaction questionnaire
Disease specific measures of patient involvement	– Diabetes empowerment scale – Patient perception of involvement in acute myocardial infarction care scale

include structural and process factors conductive to patient-centred care (such as physical barriers), organisational and team culture known to be associated with patient perceptions of care, or policies and procedures that need to be put in place in order to systematically deploy a patient-centred approach. These measures are neither widely known, implemented nor used in research (Table 2).

Existing quality improvement models and standards partly address these domains (in particular addressing issues around informed consent, patient education, and patients' rights), but they may not address them in sufficient detail. For example, a hospital quality assessment procedure may request an informed consent policy. In order for such a policy to have a real effect on patient-involvement, assessments would need to entail whether the policy has been translated into procedures to assess informed consent, whether informed consent forms exist and are up-to-date, whether they are available in different languages (if appropriate) and whether the forms are legible to patients. In addition, even though forms are comprehensible, they may be administered in awkward situation, under patient emotional stress, and, though legally sufficient, do not fully support patient-centredness. Organisational assessment tools of patient involvement provide more substantial assessments of the structures and processes that are required. They are particularly useful to support the higher order learning associate with patient involvement strategies, by

Table 2 Selected instruments to assess organisational preparedness of patient-centred care

Measure	Domains and example topics
Patient- and family-centred care: a hospital self-assessment inventory. Institute for Family Centred Care.[a]	• **Leadership**: encouraging patient-centred care in clinical practice and strategic planning. • **Mission and Definition of Quality**: includes, articulates and reflects the patient- and family-oriented care, is taught to new staff and part of continuing education. • **Charting and Documentation**: patients and families have easy access to the chart, their goals are included in the chart, they have the opportunity to record observations and concerns. • **Patients and Families as Advisors:** functioning patient and family advisory council and patients and families involved in hospital committees and task forces. • **Patient and Family Support**: staff ask patients to identify family members to participate in their care, provision of range of emotional, spiritual and practical support, peer and family-to-family support is available. • **Patterns of Care**: family can remain with patients at all times, patients and families are viewed as integral part of the health care team, open disclosure policy. • **Quality Improvement**: patients and families are involved in assessing and improving quality. • **Information/Education for Patients and Families**: patient and family involvement in decision making, range of instructional material is provided, written information in various languages. **Personnel**: patients and families are involved in recruiting and developing staff, staff assessment includes patient- and family-centred care concepts. • **Environment and Design**: welcoming first impressions, architecture and interior design, clear signage in the language of the community served, examination rooms allowing privacy and presence of family members.
Health literacy environment of hospitals and health centres. Rudd/Anderson: Harvard School of Public Health[b]	• **Navigation**: availability and easy access to telephone system, entrance, lobby, staff assistance, hallways easy to navigate, service and specialty areas. • **Print Communication**: documents prepared in clear writing style, organization and design, type style, size and contrast, photographs and illustrations • **Oral Exchange**: staff providing support and giving advice, multilingual staff available if necessary, clear communication practice including the use of audiovisual support, availability of translation services.

(continued)

Table 2 (continued)

Measure	Domains and example topics
	• **Technology**: technological components including television, telephone, computers are available and easily accessible. • **Policies & Protocols**: procedures govern the availability of print material and the provision of orientation programs for staff and volunteers, information sessions and workshops for staff address patient demographics and literacy level, staff skills building and training.
Planetree self-assessment tool. Planetree[c]	• **Human Interaction**: creating a healing environment for patients, families, and staff members. • **Family, Friends, & Social Support**: promoting caring connections between the patients and their support systems. • **Information & Education**: patients, families, and community members are provided with increased access to meaningful information. • **Nutritional & Nurturing Aspects of Food**: choice and personalized service, in combination with sound nutrition practices, add pleasure, comfort, and familiarity. • **Architectural & Interior Design**: welcoming and accessible, providing clearly marked signs for direction, comfortable and familiar rooms, and designs that engage the senses and break down barriers. • **Arts & Entertainment**: offer engagement and enjoyment by music, artwork, theatre, crafts, and clowns. • **Spirituality**: recognizing the role of spirituality in healing the whole person and meeting spiritual needs from chaplains to meditation programs. • **Human Touch**: reduce anxiety, pain, and stress through human touch, benefiting patients, families, and staff members. • **Complementary Therapies**: expand the choices offered to patients. Aroma and pet therapy, acupuncture, and Reiki are offered in addition to clinical modalities of care. • **Healthy Communities:** expand the boundaries of health care and work with schools, senior centres, churches, and other community partners.
Health Promoting Hospitals self-assessment tool. World Health Organization[d]	• **Management policy**: implement patient involvement and health promotion as part of the overall organizations' quality improvement system, including identifying responsibilities,

(continued)

Table 2 (continued)

Measure	Domains and example topics
	resources and monitoring. • **Patient information**: patients' information and health promotion needs are systematically being assessed and documented. • **Patient intervention**: patients are informed about planned activities, empowered patients for an active partnership. Patient interventions are integrated in patient pathway. • **Promoting a healthy workplace**: the hospital establishes conditions for a healthy workplace and environment, including induction programmes and maintain staff awareness on health issues. • **Continuity and cooperation**: the hospital collaborates with other health service providers and other institutions and sectors, including patients' handover.

[a] https://www.ipfcc.org/bestpractices/IPFCC_Better_Together_Self_Assessment_June_2021.pdf
[b] https://www.hsph.harvard.edu/healthliteracy/environments/
[c] https://resources.planetree.org/patient-and-family-partnership-quality-check/
[d] http://www.euro.who.int/__data/assets/pdf_file/0009/99819/E88584.pdf

questioning the assumptions underlying current organisation of care and patterns of practice.

4 Higher Order Learning in Practice: Current Uptake by Hospitals of Patient Involvement Strategies

In addition to assessing patient views and organisational characteristics and involving patients in deciding what is being measured, a fundamental next step to further supporting higher order learning is the involvement of patients in (quality) management functions. The involvement of patients and their representatives in health care in general and in quality improvement in particular takes many forms, ranging from lay membership in managerial boards to involvement in condition-specific activities, such as services design, development of patient information material, identification of improvement potentials or assessing and interpreting results of patient surveys (Institute for Family Centred Care 2009). Hospitals recognised for their leadership in the field of patient-centred care involve patients or patient representatives in such a range of formal quality functions (Conway 2008). Besides the examples from the innovators little is known about the extent to which hospitals involve patients and the public in formal quality management roles. This is in contrast to the substantial emphasis on PI in research and policy. Moreover, there is anecdotal evidence of substantial criticism among managers and clinicians regarding the role and impact of PI. It is likely that much of this does not necessary reflect a general rejection of the topic, but a lack of understanding what PI can add and how it can be implemented. Providing information that could help form such an understanding and support specific initiatives is an important objective if PI is to gain more acceptance.

4.1 Levels of Involvement of Patients in Quality Improvement Functions at Hospital and Departmental Level

We assess the actual levels of patient involvement in a variety of quality management functions in a large study of European hospitals (Box 1). The most commonly reported form of PI related to Quality Improvement Projects (20.2% of respondents reported that patients and the public were always or usually involved), followed by discussing the results of quality improvement projects (16.1%), quality committees (14.8%) and the development of quality criteria (13.5%). The least common form of involvement was regarding the design/organisation of processes; only 6.7% of respondents reported that patients and the public were always or usually involved) (Table 3). To assess whether PI differs between hospital departments, we administered the same questionnaire to heads of four departments in charge of the care for patients with acute myocardial infarction, deliveries, hip fractures and stroke.

Similar to the hospital level response, the involvement of patients and the public in the design/organisation of processes was lowest of the five scale items; however, they were almost twice as high compared to the hospital level. For individual scale items the responses at departmental level do not reflect statistically significant differences in the uptake of PI between departments. Among the four departments, PI seemed lowest in the context of stroke and hip fracture services and highest in the context of acute myocardial infarction services (Table 3).

Box 1 The Deepening Our Understanding of Quality Improvement in Europe (DUQuE) Study

The *Deepening our understanding of quality improvement in Europe (DUQuE)* project was funded by the EU 7th Research Framework Program (Groene et al. 2010). The overall aims and objectives of the project are described in detail elsewhere (Secanell et al. 2014). We draw on the results of cross-sectional survey among hospital managers and department managers from hospitals that were randomly selected in the participating countries Czech Republic, France, Germany, Poland, Portugal, Spain, and Turkey between May 2011 and January 2012. The data reported here is based on surveys to the hospital quality manager and heads of departments; responses rates were high (97% for the hospital level and >87% for the departmental level). In this sample, 74 hospitals contributed data. The majority were public hospitals (79.7%) and about half (44.5%) were teaching hospitals. Larger hospitals with more than 500 beds accounted for more than half of the hospitals in the sample.

PI was measured using a scale on the involvement of patients and their representatives in QM functions. This scale was validated and used in previous research (Groene et al. 2009). It is based on the most common ways of involving patients and the public in quality improvement and follows a Plan-Do-Check-Act cycle, in which quality standards are derived, implemented and assessed, which then leads to further improvements. The scale is based on five items, each scored on a four-point Likert scale that assess whether patients are involved in:

- the development of quality criteria/standards/ protocols,
- the design/organisation of processes,
- quality committees,
- quality improvement projects and
- discussion of results of quality improvement projects.

The scale was measured once at the hospital level and then again in four different departments in charge of providing services to patients with myocardial infarction, stroke, hip fracture, or childbirth services. We provide descriptive statistics on the implementation scores for each of the five items and use Fisher's exact test to assess whether differences exist in the implementation across clinical departments.

Table 3 Patient involvement in planning for quality at hospital and departmental levels

	Hospital wide strategies		Acute myocardial infarction		Deliveries		Hip fracture		Stroke		
Total respondents	N = 72	Valid percent	N = 64	Valid percent	N = 65	Valid percent	N = 65	Valid percent	N = 68	Valid percent	P value[a]
Development of Quality Criteria											0.211
Never	42	58.3%	22	37.9%	37	57.8%	31	50.8%	38	55.9%	
Sometimes	20	27.8%	28	48.3%	17	26.6%	19	31.1%	21	30.9%	
Usually	8	11.1%	4	6.9%	4	6.3%	8	13.1%	7	10.3%	
Always	2	2.8%	4	6.9%	6	9.4%	3	4.9%	2	2.9%	
Design/organisation of processes											0.217
Never	45	63.4%	28	47.5%	43	67.2%	36	58.1%	41	60.3%	
Sometimes	21	29.6%	24	40.7%	11	17.2%	17	27.4%	18	26.5%	
Usually	3	4.2%	5	8.5%	6	9.4%	8	12.9%	8	11.8%	
Always	2	2.8%	2	3.4%	4	6.3%	1	1.6%	1	1.5%	
Quality committees											0.276
Never	48	66.7%	30	53.6%	37	59.7%	44	71.0%	41	61.2%	
Sometimes	13	18.1%	16	28.6%	16	25.8%	10	16.1%	15	22.4%	
Usually	4	5.6%	7	12.5%	3	4.8%	2	3.2%	8	11.9%	
Always	7	9.7%	3	5.4%	6	9.7%	6	9.7%	3	4.5%	
Quality improvement projects											0.202
Never	37	51.4%	23	41.1%	37	59.7%	35	57.4%	35	52.2%	
Sometimes	20	27.8%	23	41.1%	16	25.8%	19	31.1%	20	29.9%	
Usually	9	12.5%	9	16.1%	4	6.5%	3	4.9%	9	13.4%	
Always	6	8.3%	1	1.8%	5	8.1%	4	6.6%	3	4.5%	
Discussion of quality improvement project results											0.322
Never	44	61.1%	25	46.3%	39	63.9%	37	59.7%	36	53.7%	
Sometimes	16	22.2%	18	33.3%	14	23.0%	18	29.0%	20	29.9%	

(continued)

Table 3 (continued)

Total respondents	Hospital wide strategies N = 72	Valid percent	Acute myocardial infarction N = 64	Valid percent	Deliveries N = 65	Valid percent	Hip fracture N = 65	Valid percent	Stroke N = 68	Valid percent	P value[a]
Usually	5	6.9%	10	18.5%	4	6.6%	5	8.1%	10	14.9%	
Always	7	9.7%	1	1.9%	4	6.6%	2	3.2%	1	1.5%	

[a] P-value for differences in items across pathways from Fisher's exact test

5 Strengthening Patient Involvement in Health Care in the Future

Patient involvement takes multiple forms in health care and there is not a single strategy or method that can be considered to reflect best practice (American Hospital Association 2005). This exhibits that PI is still a young field and open to experimentation. PI can serve important functions to support quality improvement efforts, in particular regarding defining how services should be provided and working with health professionals in specific projects to identity quality improvement opportunities. In contrast, the assessment of actual patient and public involvement in quality improvement in a sample of EU hospitals shows that PI is low, in particular with regard to important activities such as establishing quality standards or organising processes, for which evidence suggests that patients can make important contributions. The only area where patients and their representatives appear to be involved to some extent is regarding the implementation of quality improvement projects. This finding is systematic and observed both at hospital and departmental level. We didn't detect differences in PI at departmental level. This is an interesting finding that suggests that where realising patients' participation is more complex due to age or functional status (stroke and hip fracture patients), service providers might have found ways to involve patients after recovery or use other forms of patient representatives, such as family members or members of the public.

Our observations on the actual involvement of patients and the public are in line with recent literature from the US that, based on a survey of 112 patient-centred medical home practices in 22 states in the US, suggest that "fewer than a third of patient-centred medical home practices engage patients in quality improvement" (Han et al. 2013). These low levels of implementation contrast the range of case studies that illustrate that PI has clear benefits for service improvement. They also reflect that in practice barriers for the implementation of PI exist, in particular the (i) still prevalent assumption that patients cannot make a contribution, (ii) the threat that PI poses by potentially challenging established principles of health service organisation, (iii) the time requirements to make PI work and (iv) the lack and expertise of dedicated coordinators to make the best out of PI (Han et al. 2013; Wiig et al. 2013; Renedo et al. 2014; Thompson 2007; Fudge et al. 2008).

Currently, most studies on PI seem to rely on examples from the innovators (Luxford et al. 2011). To what extent PI impacts on service organisation at large still requires further assessment. Establishing causal pathways between levels of involvement and desired outcomes, however, is prone to a number of methodological challenges (Groene et al. 2009). The first is the time lag between PI and observing the desired outcome. PI is no quick fix and it may take months or years before processes are well established that provide a trusted environment for patients to contribute to quality improvement and a further time lag before such contributions translate into observable changes in outcome. Secondly, the wide variety of strategies employed to involve PI makes it difficult to disentangle the effect of these strategies. For example, Mockford et al. demonstrated that patient and public involvement has a range of impacts on health care services, in particular around information development and dissemination, including patient information brochures (Mockford et al. 2012). Thirdly, without a clear knowledge of the context in which PI takes place, any associational or causal analysis will be very limited. For example, patients may be involved and highly present in all phases of quality improvement work; however, without a commitment of leadership to challenge current patterns of service provision such involvement may not bear any fruits (Wiig et al. 2013).

These challenges provide a roadmap for further research on PI. Given the strong emphasis on PI by research funding organisations, the currently limited knowledge on how PI is best implemented, and the high-profile cases demanding more patient-centred care, such research seems highly warranted (Report of the Mid Staffordshire NHS Foundation Trust Public Inquiry 2013). Research should ideally use both qualitative and quantitative methods. Qualitative work is best suited to investigate the conditions under which PI is implemented and to develop or refine theory on the impact of its implementation. Quantitative research should continue to assess the extent of PI implementation and seek to analyse how this is associated with or leads to desired outcomes. Numerous factors that are potential confounders and mediators will require a robust framework for such an evaluation.

Whilst we encourage to continue involving patients in quality improvement projects and committees, service providers should also consider PI at other key stages, in particular in setting quality standards and criteria and in evaluating the results. There are lessons to be learned about the current effectiveness of strategies to improve patient involvement in their own care, but also in system design, particularly regarding the target groups for patient involvement, the role of patient representatives and the use of theory to guide interventions.

5.1 Target Those Most in Need

Quality improvement efforts that aim at involving patients may face a paradox: often, those who are more educated get involved most, understand most, ask more questions, but are those least in need. In fact, not everybody wants to be involved and in general, less educated patients tend to prefer less involvement than better educated patients (Wilkinson et al. 2008; Levinson et al. 2005). In the context of patient safety projects, it is also often assumed that patients have the desire and capacity to being proactive in asking factual (such as “when can I get back to normal”) or challenging questions (such as “did you wash your hands”) to health care staff regarding safety practices. Davies and colleagues demonstrated in a survey that challenging health care staff is less likely among men, less educated and unemployed (Davis et al. 2008), which may reinforce social gaps. Finally, those most in need may be least equipped to understand written or oral communication (Agency for Health Care Research and Quality 2004). Developers and evaluators of strategies to improve patient involvement should reflect on these findings and address the paradox that those that are most in need probably benefit least.

5.2 *Patient Representatives*

One strategy taken up by many hospitals recognised for their leadership is the involvement of patients or patient representatives in formal quality functions (such as setting standards, targets, discussing results) (Groene et al. 2009). Patients or patient representatives involved in such functions are often middle-class citizens, such as retired teachers, lawyers or members of other professions. The examples from *Dana Faber Institute* and the *Children's Hospital* in Boston in the USA provide evidence that patients make valuable contributions to quality management work. The success of patient involvement however may depend largely on being able to recruit patients with the right experience and their ability to express their views constructively (Conway 2008; Institute for Family Centred Care 2009). Thus, despite the strong policy agenda in some countries to increase patient involvement in quality improvement functions, further assessments should examine its effectiveness in terms of the type of patients performing the functions, the criteria used for their selection, the training they received to perform their functions, the contributions they make to quality improvement and the consequences of their contributions in care design. Further research should also address patients' views on these functions and how patient involvement in quality improvement might affect the professional-patient trust relationship.

5.3 *Underlying Theory*

Although there is broad literature on patient involvement care, the evidence base on which interventions are most effective in improving health outcomes needs further strengthening, partly because of the lack of clear conceptual models and lack of gold standard measures of what constitutes patient centredness. More importantly, from a health education perspective many quality improvement interventions to improve patient involvement appear to be restricted to providing health-related information. The underlying behavioural theory thus relies on the effectiveness of a rational choice theory approach in which behaviour is conditioned by cognition, which can be modified by information leaflets, educational interventions, financial incentives or patient decision aids. Health education literature demonstrates the limitations of this paradigm and suggests alternative behavioural strategies such as social cognitive theory (Bandura 2004), in which social marketing and peer modelling are key strategies to modify behaviour, or Prochaska's trans-theoretical model of change, that recognises that behavioural change requires passing different stages from precontemplation to action, which is not necessarily a linear process (Prochaska and DiClemente 1983). Thus, the underlying theoretical model should guide actual interventions to improve patient involvement.

6 Conclusion

In conclusion, the causal pathway through which patient involvement contributes to quality improvement and is associated with outcomes is very complex. From a quality improvement perspective, patient involvement strategies are justified by better meeting patients' rights, improving health outcomes, or using information provided by patients to contribute to organisational learning. With regard to the measurement strategy for patient involvement, no gold standard measure is available and measures of patient views should be accompanied by assessments of organisational policies and processes. There is a risk that strategies aiming at improving patient centredness may benefit less those with higher information needs. Interventions to improve patient-centred care should revise their conceptual and theoretical basis in order to improve their effectiveness.

References

Agency for Healthcare Research and Quality (AHRQ). 2004. *Literacy and health outcomes*. Washington.

American Hospital Association (AHA). 2005. *Patient- and Family-Centred Care: A Hospital Self-Assessment Inventory*. Washington.

Balik, B., J. Conway, L. Zipperer, and J. Watson. 2011. *Achieving an Exceptional Patient and Family Experience of Inpatient Hospital Care*. IHI Innovation Series white paper. Cambridge, MA.: Institute for Healthcare Improvement (IHI).

Balint, E. 1969. The possibilities of patient-centred medicine. *Journal of the Royal College of General Practitioners* 17: 269–276.

Bandura, A. 2004. Health promotion by social cognitive means. *Health Education and Behavior* 31 (2): 143–164.

Berwick, D. M. 2009. What 'Patient-Centered' Should Mean: Confessions Of An Extremist. *Health Affairs* 28 (4): https://doi.org/10.1377/hlthaff.28.4.w555.

Boivin, A., K. Currie, B. Fervers, J. Graica, M. James, C. Marshall, C. Sakala, S. Sanger, J. Strid, V. Thomas, T. van der Weijden, R. Grol, J. Burgers, and G-I-N Public. 2010. Patient and public involvement in clinical guidelines: international experiences and future perspectives. *Quality and Safety in Health Care*. https://doi.org/10.1136/qshc.2009.034835.

Boyer, L., P. Francois, E. Doutre, G. Weil, and J. Labarere. 2006. Perception and use of the results of patient satisfaction surveys by care providers in a French teaching hospital. *International Journal for Quality in Health Care* 18: 359–364.

van Campen, C., H. Sixma, R. D. Friele, J. J. Kerssens, and L. Peters. 1995. Quality of care and patient satisfaction: a review of measuring instruments. *Medical Care Research and Review* 52 (1): 109–133.

Conway, J. 2008. Patients and families: powerful new partners for healthcare and caregivers. *Healthcare Executive* 23 (1): 60–62.

Coulter, A., and J. Ellins. 2007. Effectiveness of strategies for informing, educating, and involving patients. *British Medical Journal* 335: 24–27.

Coulter, A., and C. Jenkinson. 2005. European patients' views on the responsiveness of health systems and healthcare providers. *European Journal of Public Health* 15 (4): 355–360.

Council of European Commission. 2010. Innovative approaches for chronic diseases in public health and healthcare systems. http://www.consilium.europa.eu/uedocs/cms_Data/docs/pressdata/en/lsa/118282.pdf. Accessed March 3, 2021.

Crawford, M. J., D. Rutter, C. Manley, T. Weaver, K. Bhui, N. Fulop, and P. Tyrer. 2002. Systematic review of involving patients in the planning and development of health care. *British Medical Journal* 325: 1263–7.

Davies, E., and P. D. Cleary. 2005. Hearing the patient's voice? Factors affecting the use of patient survey data in quality improvement. *Quality and Safety in Health Care* 14 (6): 428–432.

Davis, R. E., M. Koutantji, and C. A. Vincent. 2008. How willing are patients to question healthcare staff on issues related to the quality and safety of their healthcare? An exploratory study. *Quality and Safety in Health Care* 17 (2): 90–96.

Department of Health (DH) 2008. *High quality care for all: NHS Next Stage Review final report*. London.

Engel, G. L. 1977. The need for a new medical model: a challenge for biomedicine. *Science* 196: 129–136.

Fudge, N., C. D. Wolfe, and C. McKevitt. 2008. Assessing the promise of user involvement in health service development: ethnographic study. *British Medical Journal* 336: 313–317.

Gerteis, M., S. Edgman-Levitan, J. Daley, and T. L. Delbanco (eds). 1993. *Through the Patient's Eyes: Understanding and Promoting Patient-Centered Care*. San Francisco: Jossey-Bass.

Groene, O., K. Lombarts, N. Klazinga, J. Alonso, A. Thompson, and R. Suñol. 2009. Is patient-centredness in European hospitals related to existing quality improvement strategies: analysis of a cross-sectional survey (MARQuIS Project). *Quality and Safety in Health Care* 18: i44–i50.

Groene O, Klazinga N, Wagner C, Arah OA, Thompson A, Bruneau C, Suñol R. 2010. Deepening our Understanding of Quality Improvement in Europe Research Project. Investigating organizational quality improvement systems, patient empowerment, organizational culture, professional involvement and the quality of care in European hospitals: the 'Deepening our Understanding of Quality Improvement in Europe (DUQuE)' project. BMC Health Serv Res. Sep 24;10:281. doi: https://doi.org/10.1186/1472-6963-10-281.

Han, E., S. H. Scholl, S. Morton, C. Bechte, and R. Kessler. 2013. Survey Shows That Fewer Than A Third Of Patient-Centered Medical Home Practices Engage Patients In Quality Improvement. *Health Affairs* 32 (2): 368–375.

Hibbard, J. H., E. R. Mahoney, J. Stockard, and M. Tusler. 2005. Development and testing of a short form of the patient activation measure. *Health Services Research* 40: 1918–1930.

Hildon, Z., D. Allwood, and N. Black. 2012. Impact of format and content of visual display of data on comprehension, choice and preference: a systematic review. *International Journal for Quality in Health Care* 24 (1): 55–64.

Institute for Patient and Family Centred Care (IPFCC). 2009. *Developing and Sustaining a Patient and Family Advisory Council*. Washington (D.C.).

Institute of Medicine (IOM). 2001. *Crossing the quality chasm: a new health system for the 21st century*. Washington (D.C.): National Academies Press

Lazarus, R. S. 2000. Toward better research on stress and coping. *American Psychologist* 55 (6): 665–673.

Levinson, W., A. Kao, A. Kuby, and R. A. Thisted. 2005. Not all patients want to participate in decision making. A national study of public preferences. *Journal of General Internal Medicine* 20 (6): 531–535.

Lewin, S. A., Z. C. Skea, V. A. Entwistle, M. Zwarenstein, and J. Dick. 2001. Interventions for providers to promote a patient-centred approach in clinical consultations (review). *Cochrane Database of Systematic Reviews* (4): CD003267.

Lipkus, I. M., G. Samsa, and B. K. Rimer. 2001. General performance on a numeracy scale among highly educated samples. *Medical Decision Making* 21: 37–44.

Lorig, K. R., P. L. Ritter, A. Dost, K. Plant, D. D. Laurent, and I. McNeil. 2008. The Expert Patients Programme online, a 1-year study of an Internet-based self-management programme for people with long-term conditions. *Chronic Illness* 4 (4): 247–256.

Luxford, K., D. G. Safran, and T. Delbanco. 2011. Promoting patient-centered care: a qualitative study of facilitators and barriers in healthcare organizations with a reputation for improving the patient experience. *International Journal of Quality in Health Care* 23 (5): 510–515.

Marcus, E. N. 2006. The silent epidemic – the health effects of illiteracy. *The New England Journal of Medicine* 355 (4): 339–341.

Mid Staffordshire NHS Foundation Trust Public Inquiry. 2013. *Report of the Mid Staffordshire NHS Foundation Trust Public Inquiry. Chaired by Robert Francis QC. Executive summary.* London: The Stationery Office. http://www.midstaffspublicinquiry.com/sites/default/files/report/Executive%20summary.pdf. Accessed March 3, 2021.

Mockford, C., S. Staniszewska, F. Griffiths, and S. Herron-Marx. 2012. The impact of patient and public involvement on UK NHS health care: a systematic review. *International Journal of Quality in Health Care* 24 (1): 28–38.

Nonaka, I., and H. Takeuchi. 1995. *The Knowledge-Creating Company*. New York: Oxford University Press.

Peters, E., J. Hibbard, P. Slovic, and N. Dieckmann. 2007. Numeracy skill and the communication, comprehension, and use of risk-benefit information. *Health Affairs (Millwood)* 26 (3): 741–748.

Pfaff, H. 2004. Organisationsentwicklung und Organisationslernen im Krankenhaus [Organisational development and organisational learning in hospitals]. In *Gesundheitsökonomie, Qualitätsmanagement und Evidence-based Medicine. Eine systematische Einführung [Health economics, quality management and evidence-based medicine. A systematic introduction](in German),* eds. K. Lauterbach, and M. Schrappe, pp. 328–334. Stuttgart, New York: Schattauer.

Prochaska, J. O., and C. C. DiClemente. 1983. Stages and processes of self-change of smoking: toward an integrative model of change. *Journal of Consulting and Clinical Psychology* 51: 390–395.

Renedo, A., C. A. Marston, D. Spyrindonidis, and J. Barlow. 2014. Patient and public involvement in health care quality improvement: How organizations can help patients and professionals to collaborate. *Public Management Review* 17 (1): 17–34. https://doi.org/10.1080/14719037.2014.881535.

Roter, D., and S. Larson. 2002. The Roter interaction analysis system (RIAS): utility and flexibility for analysis of medical interactions. *Patient Education and Counseling* 46 (4): 243–251.

Schoen, C., R. Osborn, P.T. Huynh, M. Doty, K. Zapert, J. Peugh, and K. Davis. 2005. Taking the pulse of health care systems: experiences of patients with health problems in six countries. *Health Affairs (Milwood)*: W5–509–525.

Secanell, M., O. Groene, O. A. Arah, M. A. Lopez, B. Kutryba, H. Pfaff, N. Klazinga, C. Wagner, S. Kristensen, P. D. Bartels, P. Garel, C. Bruneau, A. Escoval, M. França, N. Mora, R. Suñol, and DUQuE Project Consortium. 2014. Deepening our understanding of quality improvement in Europe (DUQuE): overview of a study of hospital quality management in seven countries. *International Journal of Quality in Health Care* 26 (1): 5–15.

Selby, J. V., and S. H. Lipstein. 2014. PCORI at 3 Years — Progress, Lessons, and Plans. *The New England Journal of Medicine* 370: 592–595. doi:370:592-595.

Streiner, D. L., and G. R. Norman. 2003. Health measurement scales. 3rd ed. New York: Oxford University Press.

Sunstein, C. R., and R. H. Thaler. 2003. Libertarian paternalism is not an oxymoron. *University of Chicago Law Review* 70: 1159–1202.

Thompson, A. G. H. 2007. The meaning of patient involvement and participation in health care consultations: a taxonomy. *Social Science and Medicine* 64: 1297–1310.

Wilkinson, C., M. Khanji, P. E. Cotter, O. Dunne, and S. T. O'Keeffe. 2008. Preferences of acutely ill patients for participation in medical decision-making. *Quality and Safety in Health Care* 17 (2): 97–100.

Wiig, S., M. Storm, K. Aase, M. T. Gjestsen, M. Solheim, S. Harthug, G. Robert, N. Fulop, and QUASER team. 2013. Investigating the use of patient involvement and patient experience in quality improvement in Norway: rhetoric or reality? *BMC Health Services Research* 13: 206.

World Health Organization (WHO). 2011. *Patients for Patient Safety – How patient engagement became a priority*. Geneva http://www.who.int/patientsafety/patients_for_patient/PFPS_brochure_2013.pdf. Accessed March 3, 2021.